High Mountains & Deep Valleys
THE GOLD BONANZA DAYS

SOUTHWEST BASIN RANGE COUNTRY

DEATH VALLEY   OWENS VALLEY   HIGH SIERRA
HIGH DESERT   MINING DAYS   GHOST TOWNS
BRISTLECONE PINE MOUNTAINS   MONO BASIN

High Mountains & Deep Valleys

THE GOLD BONANZA DAYS

Lew and Ginny Clark
Color Photography by Rocky Rockwell

In Memory of:
    Billy Clark,
    Pioneer Teamster of the Golden Bonanza Days

©Lewis W. Clark & Virginia D. Clark, 1978
All rights reserved
Library of Congress Number 78-54265
ISBN 0-931532-05-1
Western Trails Publications,

P.O. Box 1697
San Luis Obispo, Ca, 93406

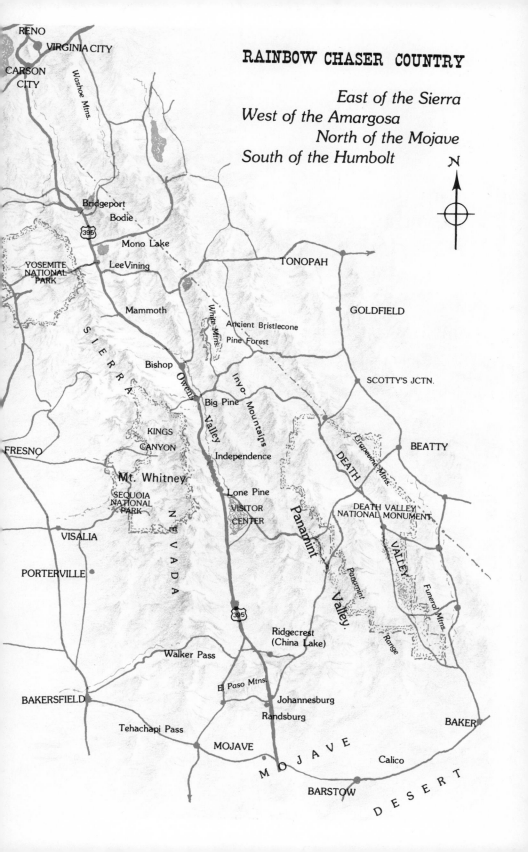

CONTENTS

THE LAND

Between the Muir-Whitney crest of the southern Sierra and the eastern slope of the Amargosa Range lies a land of great contrasts, extremes, and paradoxes. Its striking forms, climatic differences, and unusual forms of plant and animal life invited exaggerated and inventive speculations by early visitors.

In this southwestern corner of the great American Desert, once intermittently filled with inland seas and fresh water lakes, lies the Basin and Range Province. Its mountain ranges, lying along a north-west to south-east trending pattern, enclose deep depressed valleys. Lying within the rain-shadow of the Sierra its climate and strange forms of life have developed in dramatic ways. The eastward sweeping winds from the Pacific have lost most of their moisture by the time they cross the Sierra Crest. In this vast, arid region annual precipitation in the sinks averages less than 3"-4". In some areas less than ½" of rain falls—most of it evaporating as soon as it hits the ground. Moisture that does fall on the highest ridges provides many springs and small streams but they soon disappear on their downward course into deep gravel fans and basins.

Cloudbursts during the late summer account for most of the moisture. They are of short duration—a few minutes to an hour or so—and create havoc as the floods, twenty-thirty feet deep, race down the barren hills and canyons carrying everything in their way. Sweeping out over deep, rocky fans they soon disappear leaving only a few rivulets and pools to conclude their extravagant action. Old Timers warn, "Never linger in the canyons when there's thunder in the mountains."

The crests of the White-Inyo and Panamint range lie within the upper temperate zone where cold nights and occasional snow come as early as November and last well into late spring. These summits are literally islands in the sky supporting extensive, open forests of juniper, pinyon, limber, and bristlecone pine.

9

In general the Basin Range country could be characterized as a place where the tearing down forces of nature such as down-faulting, earthquakes and landslides have been assisted by cloudbursts and wind. This action has been countered by the down-faulting of its basins and the uplifting of its massive ranges exceeding 13-14,000 feet.

The White-Inyo Range is a single massive block 110 miles long with an average elevation about 10,000'. Exceptions are White Mountain Peak (14,242') and at the depressed connecting area, Westgard Pass (7276'). The White Mountains contain a dozen peaks well above 11,000' (6% over 13,000'); the Inyo Range includes a half dozen peaks above 11,000'. The rocks are intensely folded and broken by severe earth movements. The eastern front of the combined range dropping down into Saline Valley is as abrupt and majestic as that of the eastern escarpment of the Sierra.

The Panamint Range, some 60 miles long, averages well above 9500'. Its highest places are found at Tin Mountain (8953') and Telescope Peak (11,094'). Panamint Valley during glacial times was covered with a lake of some 272 square miles and 930' deep. Today, the lowest part of the valley is a playa some seventeen miles long and three miles wide. The eastern face of the Panamints is a most imposing sight viewed from Badwater (-282') or Dante's View (5476'). Its escarpment extends downward into the Death Valley sink 500' more than the towering Mt. Whitney above the Owens Valley.

East of Death Valley the Amargosa Range presents a lower profile than either the Panamint, Argus or Inyo-White mountains. Grapevine Peak (8738') is the highest point in the Grapevine Mountains while the Funeral Mountains averages well above 6000'. In the Black Mountains, Coffin Peak (5503') and Funeral Peak (6384') are the highest. The Greenwater Range stands lower, around 5000'.

Across the entire southern end of these ranges and basins, the Garlock Fault separates the above ranges from the broad Mojave Desert. Along this east-west fault between the El Paso's and Avawitz mountains, is a broken sequence of low peaks and ridges that have provided a most effective barrier to any escape of precipitation from the Basin and Range area. The Amargosa River is the most dramatic example of this. Rising northeast of Death Valley in the Bullfrog Hills it flows south through the Amargosa Desert east of the Greenwater Range, past Death Valley Junction, Shoshone and Tecopa, then, encountering the highlands of the Avawitz Mountains it turns west and north to enter Death Valley below Saratoga Springs. Continuing north between the Owlshead and Black Mountains—it flows into the lowest area of the sink between Dante's View and Telescope Peak. It is mostly an underground flow of water that appears as a "river" only in rare, wet seasons. This is typical of all desert sinks. They are quite unlike the great rivers that eroded the valleys of western America where their waters sought the ocean.

Extensive glaciers carried away to the west a great mantle of materials and deposited it in the San Joaquin Valley. Authorities hold that as much as nine vertical miles or more of overburden was removed from the Sierra block and deposited in the sea to form the foundation of today's Great Valley. Eastward flowing glaciers moved downward into the Owens Valley and Mono Basin leaving deep canyons separated by bare granite walls and lateral moraines. Terminal moraines in nearly every canyon now mark the extent of their eastward flow.

Earth movements, both vertical and horizontal, are most pronounced along the east front fault line of the Sierra. Most tremendous of such action was the earthquake in 1872 when all but two of the buildings in Lone Pine were leveled, killing 27 people. In the space of just a few moments the entire range rose vertically more than 12 feet in relation to the valley floor and, horizontally, some 20 feet! Several examples of faulting are found in Death Valley that indicate extensive movement in recent times. Most noticeable are the abrupt, stair-step breaks in the alluvial fans east of the highway between Furnace Creek and Mormon Point south of Badwater.

Volcanic activity is evident in nearly all portions of this area. Numerous lava flow formations are found in the lower Owens Valley near Little Lake. Explosive type volcanic action has left cinder cones, obsidian domes, craters, and ridges such as those in the Mammoth Mountain-Mono Crater region south of Mono Lake. In Death Valley, Ubehebe Crater provides an unusual example of explosive action.

11

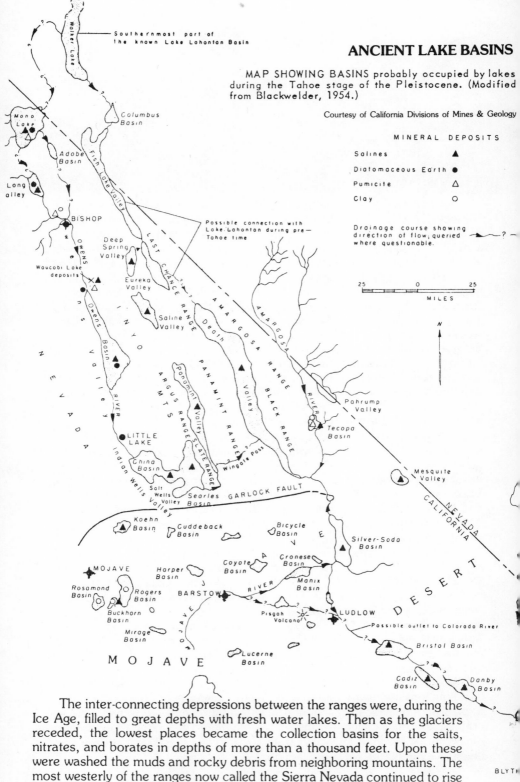

ANCIENT LAKE BASINS

MAP SHOWING BASINS probably occupied by lakes during the Tahoe stage of the Pleistocene. (Modified from Blackwelder, 1954.)

Courtesy of California Divisions of Mines & Geology

MINERAL DEPOSITS

Salines	▲
Diatomaceous Earth	●
Pumicite	△
Clay	○

Drainage course showing direction of flow; queried where questionable.

25   0   25
MILES

N

Southernmost part of the known Lake Lahontan Basin

Possible connection with Lake Lahontan during pre-Tahoe time

Walker Lake

Mono Lake

Columbus Basin

Adobe Basin

Long alley

Fish Lake Valley

BISHOP

Deep Spring Valley

Waucobi Lake deposits

Eureka Valley

Saline Valley

OWENS

Owens Basin

RIVER

N E V A D A

Indian Wells Valley

LITTLE LAKE

China Basin

Salt Wells Valley

LAST CHANCE RANGE

INYO RANGE

Death Valley

PANAMINT RANGE

ARGUS MTS RANGE

Panamint Valley

SLATE RANGE

Wingate Pass

Searles Basin

GARLOCK FAULT

AMARGOSA RANGE

AMARGOSA RIVER

AMARGOSA VALLEY

BLACK RANGE

Pahrump Valley

Tecopa Basin

Mesquite Valley

NEVADA CALIFORNIA

Koehn Basin

Cuddeback Basin

Bicycle Basin

Coyote Basin

Cronese Basin

Silver-Soda Basin

MOJAVE

Harper Basin

Rosamond Basin

Rogers Basin

Buckhorn Basin

BARSTOW

MOJAVE RIVER

Manix Basin

Pisgah Volcano

LUDLOW

D E S E R T

Possible outlet to Colorado River

Mirage Basin

Lucerne Basin

Bristol Basin

M O J A V E

Cadiz Basin

Danby Basin

BLYTH

The inter-connecting depressions between the ranges were, during the Ice Age, filled to great depths with fresh water lakes. Then as the glaciers receded, the lowest places became the collection basins for the salts, nitrates, and borates in depths of more than a thousand feet. Upon these were washed the muds and rocky debris from neighboring mountains. The most westerly of the ranges now called the Sierra Nevada continued to rise until its summits far exceeded its present 14,000′ elevation.

Buttermilk Country

Rocky Rockwell

Life zones change drastically between the basin floors supporting saltbush and sage and the upper mountain regions of juniper and pine. In a few hours of travel we observe adaptation habits covering the whole spectrum from the low desert to alpine life. The extremes of land forms, elevations, and climate have affected the development of unusual plants and creatures that have employed environmental accommodations to survive. In the lower basins reversed seasons take place—plants drop their leaves in summer to avoid loss of moisture from the burning sun, and their growing season is from December to May.

From the smallest mini-flower in Death Valley to the crests of the White Mountains, with their 4000 year old bristlecone pines, are found evidences where adversity has provided many unique forms of life. Drastic conditions of soil and climate have reduced their competitors for space and ensured their growth.

Where in the higher life zones the marmot and deer forage in the daylight, the basic shyness and nocturnal habits of most desert creatures leads one to believe they are non-existent. Yet tracks are found in the sand dunes or near springs in early morning. Only the very patient are fortunate enough to see the extensive wildlife activity found in the desert basin range regions. By remaining quiet in the dry sage or creosote flats you may see a lizard scurry, or a rabbit go from bush to bush or even a variety of birds.

This southwest corner of the Basin and Range country provides a unique experience for the learned or student geologist in search of nature's story; to historians retracing the quest of the Rainbow Chasing prospectors in these stark, barren hills; or the rock hunter, archeologist, ghost town explorer, or today's family in their RV's escaping from over-urbanization. All seek solace in the depths of its quietness, the beauty of the multi-colored hills, and are awed by the vastness of its clear, starlit sky.

THE RAINBOW CHASERS

The Basin and Range Province had been a land to be avoided. The search of the beaver men for furs; the pathfinders, looking for mythical Buenaventure River flowing to the western sea; the adventurers on their way to the goldfields; the pioneers seeking free land to California; even Kit Carson, Fremont and Joseph Walker—all passed this region by. The tales of those who did cross here were varied only in the details of the tragic 49'ers and the barrenness of the land.

As the Sierra's western slopes became preempted by miners and big developers, the opportunities for finding new strikes rapidly seemed to fade. Remembering some of the tales they had heard, prospectors began drifting east back over the Sierra. Discoveries of gold and silver at Virginia City and silver at Cerro Gordo set off a new rush such as the west had never seen. This time the rush was eastward. Thousands came by ship to Los Angeles and San Francisco and crossed the mountains. Mark Twain in *Roughing It* graphically relates his experiences in the mining boom camps and his passage between San Francisco and Virginia City.

Reports began drifting in that there was treasure in the desert ranges— perhaps another Comstock! Here was the setting for the "Last Hooraw of the Rainbow Chasers". They seemed to thrive in it. With ground temperatures reaching well over 150° in summer and below freezing in the winter they hold up in dugout caves near the occasional spring. They scratched along the dry ravines for tell-tale traces of gold particles, then followed them to outcropping ledges high on canyon walls. Promising samples were hurried off to the assay offices for evaluations. With good reports they usually sold out to mining men with capital behind them. With poor reports they would move on hopeful for a better find in the next canyon. Gold fever, it was called, and it spread like an incurable disease to be cured only in the finding or leaving their bones in the open desert or to lie in lonely graves among the creosote.

At first, returns from the El Paso, the Inyo's, and the Panamints were meager—usually made by *dry-washing* in open bottom gulches. It was always thin pickings. If what looked like a good strike faded, the men used up all they had made to sink newer shafts and drive deeper tunnels.

14

When they ran out of sweat, money, and hope, they moved on. Ironically, many an old abandoned mine paid rich dividends to those who came along later with new equipment or a broader knowledge of mineral wealth. For example, gold prospectors were committed to look for *gold*. Men died in poverty on claims that were rich in other ores. In the Rand Mountains thousands of men had crossed and recrossed the region later to be found rich in silver at the Kelly Mine, and tungsten at Atolia.

Shallow, placer mining was inevitably followed by hardrock miners with heavy machinery to secure and process the ore. By the mid-1900's most of the mines were pretty welll worked out. The desert became quiet again except for an exploratory blast by a newcomer here and there. A few mines were reopened or tailings reworked when higher prices of minerals made it profitable.

Now, and for several past decades, most of the mining activity has been large scale operations in the soft-ore field such as talc, salts, nitrates, and borax. It is a new age in operating, employing Geiger counters, and sophisticated detectors from helicopters. Gigantic earth-moving equipment used in open-pit mines are producing changes in the landscape greater than the volcanic built Ubehebe Crater or cloudbursts carving gorges in the washes of the desert ranges.

> The burro prospectors are gone,
> Mining towns have become ghost towns
> And the ghost towns are but symbols on our maps.
> But the legends of that great *Hooraw Time* in the Old West lives on.
> We visit the *coyote diggings,* the open shafts,
> And view the sage and sand—or follow
> Old ruts across the desert where once
> The long-line teams hauled their gold.
> —Now and then, on a furnace-hot day,
> We watch the twisting *dust devils* drift across the valley
> And see the mirage of a lake not really there.
> Then, in memory the burro-prospector and ghost town
> Live again!

Carl Mengel and His Dog
NPS Photo

15

THE ARRIVAL OF THE STEAM ENGINE

Very few strikes have been made right next to a highway or railroad. They persist in being off in the hills somewhere that takes a lot of walking and some discomforts a man wouldn't let himself in for if he had 20-20 foresight. To develop a claim required tremendous quantities of supplies that had to be hauled in by freight teams. Even the mules contributed to the problem. In most cases it took one-third to one-half of all payloads to haul enough feed and water to keep the mules going. They almost ate themselves out of business. The mule teams couldn't keep up with the needs to haul ore to railheads and supplies to the mines. Railroads had to be built along the north-south basins with railhead junctions on the east-west transcontinental route.

While it lasted it became in itself, a tough, lucrative way of life to thousands of men who never saw the inside of a mine. The first major freight route out of Tonopah was to Sodaville, a siding on the Carson and Colorado Railway. Huge wagons were built that could handle 20 tons of freight. They required 18-20 animals to haul them and make the trip in two days. In 1901 some observers reported at least 300 horses and mules were hauling between Tonopah and Goldfield. By 1905 the numbers increased to more than 2000 head. It was a payload both ways for the outfits—ore going out and supplies coming in.

Even then the freighters couldn't handle it all. Tons and tons of rich, sacked ore were stacked at the desert sidings awaiting railcars. Likewise stacks of mining equipment, timber, and household goods, awaited shipment out of such railheads as Reno, Sodaville, and Las Vegas. Railroads were extended to handle the backlog of shipments. Actually, the railroad problem was taken care of dramatically by the boom town suddenly collapsing from lack of paydirt.

GOLD FEVER ... PROSPECTORS ... GRUBSTAKES

No one ever accused the desert prospectors of living a luxurious life—except now and then the big spree after a strike. But no one can deny that as a breed they led an interesting one. Joe Otto was no exception. Living alone in a rock walled shanty up Marble Canyon in the Argus Range he persisted on his galena silver claim when most others would have quit and moved on. Years passed before he developed it enough to reveal a good show.

Then, a San Berdoo man stopping in Trona one day saw some of his silvery ore and headed for Marble Canyon. A few days later Otto showed up at The Tanks Stage Station and said he'd sold out for over $50,000 and that we was going "outside" for a spell. He wanted us to take care of his burros. We never saw him again as we also moved away from the desert.

Often we wondered how he made out in the big city after so many years being a recluse at his Ophir Mine. Years later when talking to Ed Teagle at his Stockwell Mine, I heard the rest of Joe Otto's story. It seemed that Otto went down to see the bright lights around the Hollywood area. He encountered a new kind of prospector—a lonesome widow, and they got married. It didn't take too long before the mine speculator worked out the Ophir Lode and departed for more promising fields. It didn't take much longer for Otto to discover his new claim was a phony and headed back to prospect for another Ophir—minus his bride and the $50,000.

Ed Teagle was retired and well along in years when we last saw him. He had run feed warehouses, stores, and had long forgotten how many Rainbow Chasers he had grubstaked. Now he was back at one of his old worked-out mines trying to make a grubstake on his own. Living on black coffee, a sack of flour and a side of bacon, he was still excited about his "prospects". Wouldn't let us go until we went down the shaft to take a look at what he had found. The sparkle in his eyes was brighter than our old headlamps as he dug out samples and we gathered to inspect the shiny glint in the crushed rock. He had the gold fever again for sure! One never really gets over it. Like I say, no one can deny, they led an interesting life!

EXPLORING THE EL PASO AND RAND MOUNTAINS

REDROCK CANYON

Redrock Canyon, cutting through the El Paso Mountains, is a very appropriate entry to the Basin and Range country east of the Sierra. Its colorful, sculptured cliffs rising abruptly out of the broad desert invites exploration. A number of backcountry dirt roads lead to the uplands of the El Paso Range where old mines and interesting land forms and colors entice the photographer as well as the geologist. A good campground at the Redrock Canyon State Recreation Area encourages a rest stop or overnight stay.

The uplifted front of the Garlock fault stands like a Chinese Wall facing the Mojave Desert to the south. This front reveals examples of earth movements where areas of soft, colorful sediments lie adjacent to hard, dark rock formations. The alternate layers of light colored clay, bright red sandstone and volcanic materials now exposed provides a "geologist window" to look into the past.

In the late 1800's and early 1900's when extensive mining activities required large quantities of heavy machinery and tools, the dry wash through Redrock became a scene of almost continuous activity. Supplies for the Owens Valley, Cerro Gordo, and the Panamints passed through here from Bakersfield, Ventura and Los Angeles. In this canyon was an overnight way-station for the long-line teamsters going north or south. Hay and grain was stockpiled and water from springs or shallow wells was available. Millions of dollars of the Silver Queen's treasure was brought out through here. It was a heroic task for both man and beast. Redrock was a respite sorely needed from the summer heat and the winter's ice-laden winds. Stock was rested or replaced, wagon tires reset and tall tales that became legends were exchanged around the sage stump campfires.

18

The most interesting story was that told of the time the teamster of a long-line outfit failed to heed the rumblings of thunder in the mountains and was caught in the narrows of the deep canyon. Loaded to capacity with great silver ingots from Cerro Gordo, the whole outfit—men, mules, wagons, and silver bullion rolled, tumbled, and was buried by the savage flood so deep no trace of them was ever found.

The tale, told and retold around smoky campfires became history. Or was it only a legend based upon a dream that hadn't really happened? But it did make good narrating for the "I-want-to-believe-it" listeners. There is the report that two silver bars like those hauled from the Cerro Gordo were found years later by a surveyor scouting for the Los Angeles Aqueduct project. Could the rest still be there waiting for another wayward rampage of nature to retrace and uncover an old channel now hiding a great pile of treasure? Who knows? In a land where nightfall brings out the myriad of stars, the call of the coyote and the hoot of an owl along the canyon walls, even the unbelievable might become fact and a new legend born for those who want to believe.

With the passing of decades the mines faded and the old wagons road ruts were filled with wind-driven sand. Cloudbursts roared down the canyons and carried away evidence of man's short stay here. However, new legends were born on film as Redrock Canyon became the old west's "Apache land". It was used as the setting for the locale of many old Hollywood "westerns" where stage coaches were robbed at the pass, cowboys chased cattle or Indians, and shoot-outs saved the honor of honest men.

EL PASO MOUNTAINS

The El Paso Mountains are interesting as both vertical and horizontal geologic action took place here. The Garlock fault, with its general east-west course, terminates the Basin Ranges with great vertical displacements of ancient sedimentary materials. Horizontal shifting of the land was as much as thirty to forty miles. Faulting can be seen on alluvial fans between the El Paso Canyons and the highway between Cantil and Garlock. The steep, loose fans near Goler Well shows recent uplifting fault action across its face while nearby are large depressions formed by down-faulting. Erosional forces of wind and water have removed the softer layers beneath the harder, overflow caps. Within the layers are found many evidences of prehistoric non-marine fossils. They include some of the oldest mammals in fossils found in California. Commercial miners of "soft" ores such as seismotite, bentonite, clay, borox, and salt had been attracted to the El Paso region. Well-known among them were the makers of Holly and Old Dutch Cleanser.

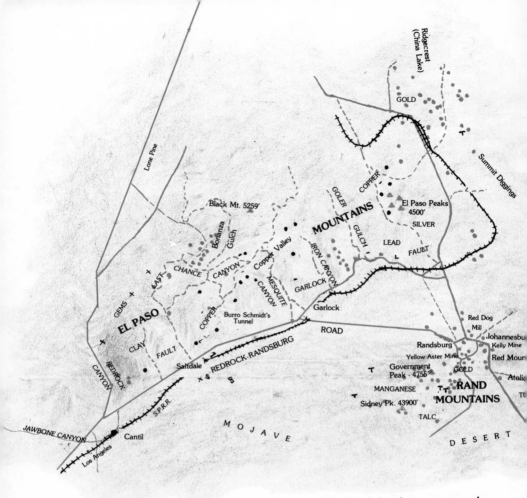

Ridgecrest (China Lake)

GOLD

Lone Pine

Summit Diggings

Black Mt. 5259'

COPPER

El Paso Peaks 4500'

SILVER

MOUNTAINS

GOLER

GULCH

Bonanza Gulch

LAST CHANCE

CANYON

Copper Valley

IRON CANYON

LEAD

FAULT

MESQUITE CANYON

GARLOCK

GEMS

COPPER

Burro Schmidt's Tunnel

Garlock

ROAD

Red Dog Mill

EL PASO

Randsburg

Johannesbu Kelly Mine

CLAY

FAULT

Yellow Aster Mine

Red Moun

Saltdale

REDROCK-RANDSBURG

Government Peak - 4756'

GOLD

Atolia

REDROCK CANYON

MANGANESE

RAND MOUNTAINS

Tu

Sidney Pk. 43900'

TALC

JAWBONE CANYON

S.P.R.R.

Cantil

MOJAVE

DESERT

Los Angeles

In the more than fifty square miles of jumbled backcountry early prospectors filed scores of claims. Today's weekend prospectors find dozens of old mining trenches, pits, and tailing dumps. Empty holes and old rusty machinery are silent testimonials to the struggle and frustrations of these early times.

Gold strikes began as far back as the 1860's but they were of small importance. Returns were meager, water was almost non-existent for any mining development so the prospectors moved on deeper into the Basin Ranges looking for the Big One. New seekers followed them, convinced there must be treasure in the El Paso's. Larger strikes were made in the late 1890's. Numerous rich pockets of good sized nuggets were found. Old trails became primitive wagon roads as the hills were invaded. Again, the prospects failed to produce enough to meet the expense of heavy mining machinery needed to work the area. Miners soon drifted away leaving their diggings for better places.

Today's weekend miners, desert buffs, and rockhound addicts find much to attract them looking for such treasures as bits of agate, jasper, opal, white quartz flecked with gold, petrified wood, and numerous fossils including those of ancient camels and horses. Some come just to poke around and take pictures of old diggings.

LAST CHANCE CANYON: Entry is fourteen miles north of Redrock Canyon off Hwy. 14. Good dirt desert road leads up into the low hills. Numerous mines are in the area. This is a very interesting trip. Side road (tracks) up Bonanza Gulch may be questionable for vehicles. Check before driving up there. Exit down to the Redrock-Randsburg road is closed.

BURRO SCHMIDT'S TUNNEL

William Schmidt started out as a part-time prospector who worked in the Kern River country in the summer and, for his health, worked in his mine diggings in the Copper Basin in the winter. The climate and work did wonders for his health as he started a tunnel in 1906 and finished it in 1938—more than three decades later. It was 5′x7′ wide and 2000′ long. His only means of transportation to and from the town of Randsburg for supplies was a team of burros, so he was known as Burro Schmidt. He used a pick, shovel, and some dynamite. The rubble was loaded in an ore car, then pushed out on a track to his dump. All this digging kept him out of trouble but never produced him a grubstake. His idea was to save hauling copper ore over the rough mountainous country. From where? To where? Only Burro Schmidt knew. As he worked his tunnel he sold off all his mining claims and had little need for it by the time he had finished.

Explorations along the old roads in Pleasant Valley, Last Chance and Mesquite canyons have many rewards for rockhounding or desert photography. All the roads in the region are unimproved and, in some places, little more than wheel tracks in sandy washes. Travel on such roads can be hazardous—especially after wind storms or summer cloudbursts. Don't travel through here unless your vehicle is in good condition, your road information is updated, and you let others know where you are going and when you expect to come out. Entry can best be made from the west and north off Hwy. 14. The roads in the gulches leading down the south front of the range to connect with the Redrock-Garlock road are steep, rough, and frequently blocked by washout debris.

Arrastre at Garlock

MESQUITE CANYON: This area can be reached from the north via upper Last Chance Canyon, east of Bonanza Gulch. There are two entries from the south—one at Garlock and one just west of Mesquite Springs. These join about a mile and a half north of the Randsburg-Garlock junction. The route follows up the narrow canyon for several miles passing some old mines along the way including the Badger, Decker and the Colorado Camp. Across the road from the latter is a low-grade coal deposit. Most of the claims have not been worked for years. Above the coal deposit the road is definitely a 4x4 trail.

To the west of Gerbracht Camp junction are the Copper Basin mines and the site of old Burro Schmidt's tunnel some two-and-a-half miles farther up the mountain. Exit from this region can be made by continuing west some five miles from Copper Basin to join the Last Chance Canyon Road.

Gold was found in Mesquite Canyon in the early 1800's. Burro pack trains loaded with the highest grade ore wound their way down the steep rocky canyon to the Garlock mills. However, even though no large strikes were made, hopeful dreamers worked the area intermittently into the early 1900's. Copper, gold, galena (silver-lead) and even coal was found but only in limited quantities.

GARLOCK

The town of Garlock (originally called El Paso City or Cow Wells) enjoyed its boom days in the late 1800's when a stamp mill was brought in from Tehachapi and began working out ores from some of the scores of small diggings scattered in the El Paso's as far east as the Summit Range and south to the Rand Mountains. With plenty of water here and the many claims being developed, some half dozen mills worked almost around the clock to accommodate the loads delivered by the freight teams

At its height Garlock boasted several hundred people and a business center with post office and doctor's office. Many people did not actually work in the mines but fared well on the goods needed and services they provided. Business operations included a boarding house, hotel, general store, barber and drug store, with of course, the "recreation center" at Millers Bar. One important service was the hauling of water and mining equipment by the freighters.

As the El Paso mines became worked out and new strikes were made south in the Rand Mountains, Garlock began to fade. Then, for a time, the first rich ores of the Yellow Aster Mine required more milling than Garlock could handle so the Yellow Aster built its own 50-stamp and 100-stamp mills. Added to the loss of this source of revenue in milling was that of hauling water. Pipe line and pumps were installed at Iron Canyon Wells to supply the booming town of Randsburg. Within a short time Garlock was reduced to a handful of people as buildings were dismantled "lock, stock, and barrel" and moved up the hill to the new towns of Randsburg and Johannesburg. Around 1909 Garlock became an active railroad station stop on the Southern Pacific. People from Johannesburg and Randsburg took the train to Mojave then transferred to Los Angeles or San Francisco. The Red Rock Railroad out of Mojave was built to supply the construction of the Los Angeles Aqueduct. A flash flood wiped out all but a small part of the old roadbed. So the new route went up to Cantil, east of Garlock, Searles Station, around the El Paso Mountains then north to Inyokern.

Garlock Today

The El Paso Mountains culminate in the general area of the four El Paso peaks at the northeastern end of the range. Near them were some half dozen copper mines, seven lead and silver mines, and more than two dozen gold mines.

Evidences of the scattered search for a new bonanza are found throughout the eastern El Paso region. In Iron Canyon only a few old ore dumps are left. Goler Gulch has been invaded by wind driven sands and flood debris. Little remains of the old mining tunnel there. A few old sites of the Summit Diggings where gold and glory was a flash-in-the-pan affair in the late 1890's are but empty holes in the sage. Ventures into any of these ravines and washes are low in historic interest and high in risks involved.

John Goler was a member of the '49ers Party that wandered out of Death Valley and lived not only to tell about it but also to return to the desert to search for gold he had seen in the El Paso Mountains. For two decades he worked as a blacksmith in the San Fernando and Los Angeles area. Always remembering gold he had seen, he made repeated trips back along his route out of Death Valley to try and find where it was, but without success.

Others, intrigued by his tales of gold nuggets in the hills to the east began extensive prospecting there. In 1893 gold was found in a little canyon so much like the one Goler described in his story the miners agreed it should be called Goler Canyon. A few large nuggets were all that was necessary to start a stampede to the area. Prospectors swarmed over the hills like a band of thirsty sheep looking for water. Dry washing camps soon sprang up at Last Chance, Redrock, Jawbone Canyon and Summit Diggings. It turned out to be a fine-gold placer area with little water to assist the mining. As so often in such diggings, deposits were scattered, shallow, and soon played out. The first hastily erected buildings at Goler were of canvas and stone caves and housed some 200 prospectors and miners. Later, at the peak of the rush more than 1000 men were in the nearby hills, each hoping *this* would be the big strike. A mill was even built to handle their ores, but in 1894 as Garlock had a stamp mill and more water, operations were moved down to there. True to pattern, only a few got in on the big money and the rest were lucky if they got enough to move to some place else.

RANDSBURG—JOHANNESBURG

Randsburg Today   El Paso Mountains in Background

The unpromising hills to the south attracted little attention. As yet they hadn't even been named. Then a series of events began to take place that were to change everything. Two partners, John Singleton and F.M. Mooers had lucked out at Summit as far as anything big was concerned. Mooers suggested that they go south and take another look around where he found a few evidences of gold the year before. Having only a little equipment and no means of hauling their supplies, they talked another prospector, Charlie Burcham (who had a team and wagon) to go with them. Charlie, although a somewhat reluctant companion to the venture, finally agreed to go along. Assuming the role of discouraged men that were fed up with the area, they left Summit Diggings and drove north. After being sure they were not followed they circled back south through the hills and gullies to where Mooers had prospected before.

Here, on the rough slope of what is now Rand Mountain they set up camp. From there they could look to the west to the El Paso Mountains and north to the Summit Range where so little reward had been given for the past miserable winter's toll. Their very first effort struck pay dirt! The site was to become the "Glory Hole" of the Yellow Aster Mine producing $200,000 per month and a total of more than $12 million before it closed.

The partners knew they needed money to develop what they had found. Mooers and Singleton stayed at the claim while Burcham headed for San Bernardino to get supplies and financing. He returned to the claims with both, plus his wife—Dr. Rose Burcham. She had given up her doctor's practice in San Bernardino to live in a tent in the desert hills and lend a hand. Over the years that followed that "hand" was to be felt in forceful ways as legal and financial troubles plagued their new Yellow Aster Mine and Milling Company and schemers tried to horn in on the action at Rand Camp. Claims and men covered the surrounding hills in all directions. A large share of the credit for successful struggle to develop the mine and protect their interests from conniving sharpies was due to Rose Burcham. They didn't want to sell out to some speculator for a quick profit of a few thousand dollars.

24

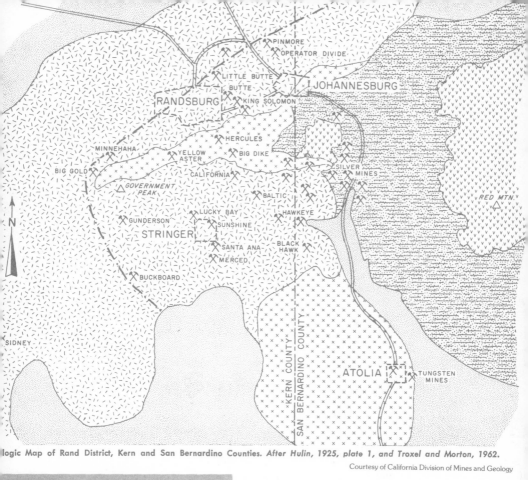

logic Map of Rand District, Kern and San Bernardino Counties. *After Hulin, 1925, plate 1, and Troxel and Morton, 1962.*

Courtesy of California Division of Mines and Geology

Francilu Hansen

During the Glory Hole days, Randsburg and Johannesburg developed into unique types of mining towns. Actually they were one community with only a low ridge separating them physically. The wealth of the Yellow Aster and the size of its operations was too great to allow the kind of lawlessness that had flourished in Ballarat, Bullfrog and Bodie. Randsburg was a company town where such way-out conduct was soon stopped. Tinhorn gamblers, the rowdies, and the lawbreakers were invited (told) to leave town. In turn, the company was progressive in its concern for the welfare of its workers and people of the town who gave it their support.

A short line railroad spur was extended from Kramer to Johannesburg to haul in the heavy machinery needed for the Yellow Aster. Kramer was on the main line of the Santa Fe from Los Angeles to Las Vegas. Randsburg with its own huge stamp mills became a bustling mining town while Johannesburg became the railhead and transportation center for all types of supplies needed to keep not only Randsburg but also other mining communities—Trona, Ballarat and Skidoo serviced.

The arrival of the railroad in 1898 changed the course of the miners' lives. As time passed and the clamor for claims calmed down the rough and ready saloon-haunt miners were replaced by men who arrived by train with their families. The presence of women and children soon made their influence felt. Schools, churches, lodge halls, and business establishments were built to serve this new type of family worker. The arrival of the daily afternoon train with its mail, supplies and tone of civilization gave the citizenry an acceptable social atmosphere. These two towns became typical of many of the frontier towns after the excitement and insecurity of their discovery days were over.

Of the many old mining centers in the Mojave Desert, Randsburg has become one of our best preserved "ghost towns". Most of its original buildings have been destroyed by repeated fires. Its early people have long gone on their last prospecting trips. The few old timers there today, with only a few exceptions, actually are newcomers who went there after the mining boom days to do a bit of prospecting or find a quiet, low-key place to live on a modest income. There is enough activity to support a few small shops, post office, church and an elementary school.

The old mines are worked out. Most of the mills have been dismantled or destroyed by firebug vandalism. Along the west end of its main street the original mining-day-buildings stand between Otto Rinaldi's Market, the Museum, and the White House. Its population includes some 125-150 residents who really like it and lead a life here little affected by the influx of large numbers of spring weekend or Christmas-time winter vacationers. More than 50 mines of early days are listed in the Rand Mining District report of the Bureau of Mines. Most of them producing gold were in the western part of the district. The eastern mines were mainly silver. Tungsten was found in large quantities at Atolia. Just south at Boron, near Kramer, borax is being mined in large scale open pits today. But that is another story.

Yellow Aster Stamp Mill

With all the excitement produced by the numerous gold discoveries over the years it followed that the prospectors' concentration of gold blinded them to other minerals until one day, a chance rest stop of two men revealed ores that assayed out to be rich in silver. This discovery in 1919 led to one of California's most famous silver booms in a region already well known for its production of gold and tungsten. Prospectors and mine workers poured in from all over the state. Johannesburg again was very active.

The Red Mountain area mines, of which the Kelly was the richest, was to produce fortunes for those who knew silver when they saw it and despair to those who had sought gold. Following this era of silver, returns from the mines of the Rand District—mines such as Sunshine, Black Hawk, Operation Divide, King Solomon, Buckboard, Little Butte and Santa Anas—dwindled. In 1933 the Santa Fe railroad tracks were torn out between Johannesburg and Kramer marking the end to the extensive mining in this district.

King Soloman Mine, Johannesburg

Johannesburg

It was in the spring of 1906 that my father, William (Billy) Clark, arrived in Johannesburg with his family—there were three older girls and two older boys in the family beside me. I don't remember much about that overland journey from Lake County—being the age of two.

Upon his arrival in Johannesburg he soon had a team and began hauling ore from the mines to the Red Dog Mill. A partnership was formed with Otto Rinaldi, a merchant of Randsburg. They bought out the freight and stage line between Johannesburg and Skidoo. Rinaldi and Clark carried mail, passengers, feed and supplies with stagecoaches and long-line freight teams between the railhead at Johannesburg to the mines extending beyond Searles Lake, the Slate Range, and the Panamints. The partnership lasted until World War I times when Fords and Moreland trucks began competing with the freight teams and stages to Ballarat and Skidoo. A new day had arrived in desert transportation.

Shortly after selling out the business and moving away to farm in the San Joaquin valley, we read of a rich silver strike being made at Red Mountain. Later, reminiscing around a Sierra campfire, Dad told me: "I was hauling through the area east of Joburg near Red Mountain. It was a cold winter's morning and I had been walking alongside of the wheelers to keep warm. Stopping the team for a short rest I found some interesting looking ore. Putting some of it in an old sack I threw it into the jocky-box under the seat thinking I would have one of the boys give it a look later. But, I never got around to it. You know, that should have been about where the boys discovered the Kelly Mine ore."

Johannesburg School House

Dick and Jane hadn't arrived yet on the educational horizon and we missed out on "See Spot Run". But we were well integrated with all ages and grades in the one room that got pretty hot in late spring. Reading, writing, and numbers covered most everything with a variation of spring picnic trips in the flower-covered hills back of the Red Dog Mill. Christmas programs brought out the grown-ups to share the pinyon pine tree decorated with popcorn balls and strings and to join in the community sing followed by Santa.

On real hot days the doors and windows were left open. Lizards slipped in to lie on the wet floor under the water cooler and the burros hung around for shade and handouts from lunch scraps. The fence was needed to keep them from joining us inside. Everyone took part in the janitor work keeping the place liveable. All in all it was a good arrangement that didn't cost too much. School gave the mothers a break, as they didn't have to worry about us falling down a mine shaft someplace.

"Uncle" Tom Duke hauled coal and would leave an extra load at the school in the winter. His favorite story about one teacher, Crazy Kate, got to be quite a legend. It seemed she kept a "45" in her desk drawer and on occasion exhibited it effectively when self-appointed citizens approached the school to tell her how to run it. Ed Teagle, who had the grocery store then, confirmed the story in later years and added: "In fact, once when I went up to the school trying to patch things up between Kate and a disgruntled father, I had my baptism of fire. Just as I got to the front gate she told me that was far enough and put a bullet in the wall over the door. I got the message. Later, several of the fellows and I returned. While she was busy watching the front, one of them slipped quietly in the back door and got the gun. Then we forcefully loaded her and her trunk on the evening train for Los Angeles."

31

FUN AND GAMES

With no television, no organized after-school programs, swimming pools or little league baseball, we had to make our own fun such as—

1. Rounding up a few prospector's burros and riding them without benefit of bridle or ropes until we got dumped off.
2. A bunch of us boys dragging a stripped down buggy-frame up the hill to the end of the road near the school. Then we would pile on and with the oldest boy steering the rig with a long rope, and the rest of us screaming our heads off we rattled down hill on main street, past the depot, Harrison's saloon, Teagle's store, past the hotel, across the present Hwy. 395, and landed up below the Red Dog Mill. Dust flying behind us!
3. Shooting tin cans off rocks with our sling-shots.
4. Collecting beer bottles—Storekeeper Ed Teagle was a soft touch. He rewarded us with chunks of hard candy.
5. "Inspecting" the loading of long-line freight outfits at the railroad depot —wondering what it was like out there beyond the big turn at Red Mountain on the way to Ballarat and Skidoo.
6. Racing to the depot to meet the in-coming train when its whistle and black smoke heralded its approach around the Atolia bend.
7. Hanging around the blacksmith shop watching Hefty Livingston wrestle a big mule into submission to be shod or shape a new red-hot steel tire to fit the wheel of an outgoing freight wagon.
8. Meeting with Mother on summer evenings counting the bright stars over Red Mountain and admiring the splendor of Haley's Comet that out-shone them all.
9. Throwing tin cans down old mine shafts and listening to their clattering on the walls until they hit bottom, wondering how many rattlesnakes were down there.
10. Watching the bartender getting ready for the evening's action— counting tall stacks of bright ten and twenty dollar gold pieces.
11. Building a long-line freight outfit. The horses were beer bottles. (My mother was a WCTU'er and no whiskey bottles could be used.) Wagon bodies were built of cigar boxes from the hotel pool room. Wheels were empty thread spools cut in half.

Francilu Hansen

Fourth of July was quite an event in Randsburg

I watched the celebration from this vantage point at the head of Butte Street. The only business going on was the business of having a good time. Events began at daybreak when a couple of miners set off a huge dynamite blast that shook the town. It was time to start celebrating! The morning was taken up with kids races, feats of strength by mine workers, renditions by the local band, and a lot of general foofaraw—mainly going from one social center to another.

The tug-of-war was an annual affair between the Yellow Aster millmen and the miners. Ladders were spliced together long enough to accommodate the two teams and placed in the center of the street. The teams sat on the ladder facing each other, with their heels locked under the rung. The heavy tug-rope was looped around the anchor men at each end. A red flag, marking the center of the rope was placed in the center of the ladder. A shot marked the beginning and end of the timed best 2-out-of-3 pulls. Losers bought the drinks for the winners.

Nearby was a tall, smooth pole that had been coated with a good amount of wagon-wheel grease. On its top was fastened a $10 gold piece. Kids took turns trying to climb the greased pole. The smart ones greased their hands and legs and then covered themselves with sand to give them friction on the pole. Other events included foot and three-legged races, burro races, and a drillers contest to see who could bore the deepest hole in a rock. A bored-hole rock now is beside the Randsburg museum. The day was concluded by fireworks display "imported all the way from Los Angeles!" The people of Randsburg worked hard and they celebrated hard and the Fourth of July topped them all.

33

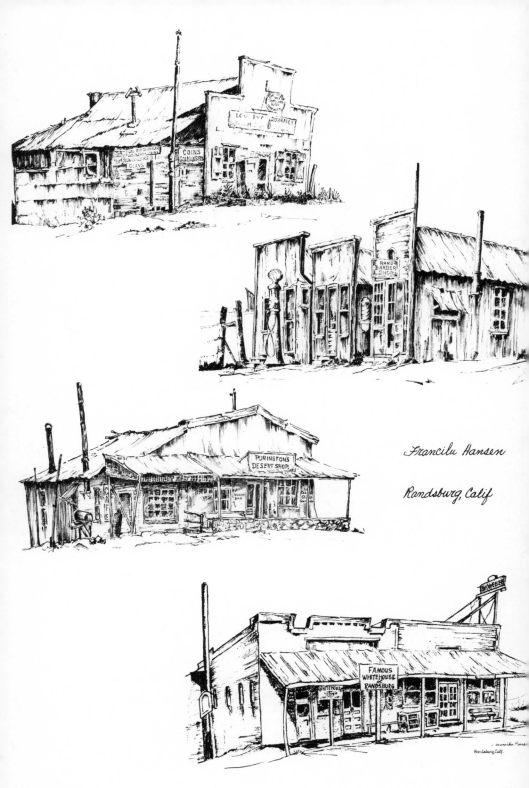

Francilu Hansen

Randsburg, Calif.

34

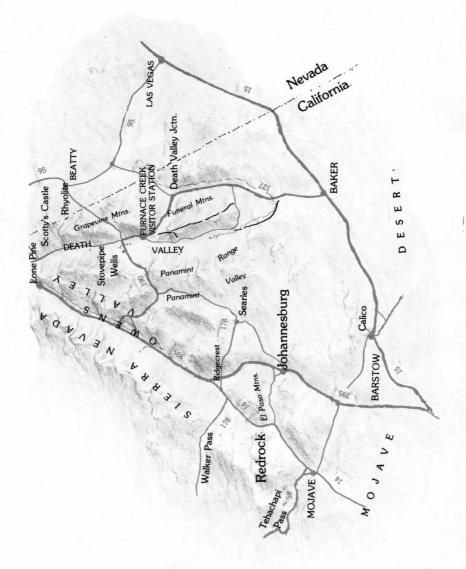

BARSTOW — HIGH DESERT COUNTRY

Since early days Barstow was the supply center to the many mining districts in the Mojave Desert. When railroads were built, it became the rail center between Los Angeles, Las Vegas, and Salt Lake City.

BARSTOW WAY STATION (Off I-15 at Barstow Road Interchange. Open seven days a week.)

The Bureau of Land Management offers information and maps of desert roads for both conventional cars and ORV's, with camping areas, interesting points, and of the hazards that could be encountered. At the Station the exhibits include natural history, desert ecology and environment, with wildflower and wildlife displays.

There are many recreational things to do in the region between Johannesburg and Barstow: visiting ghost towns, archeological sites, limestone caverns, the Sand Dunes Recreation Site, viewing Indian stone writings, and enjoying high desert camping. Rockhound enthusiasts, history buffs, and those seeking desert vacation experiences will find a wide variety to choose from. This is a winter recreation region. It is subject to extreme heat and windstorms in spring and summer. Check on weather conditions, roads, as well as your car and supplies when planning and making trips into this country.

There are many other mines east of Barstow and north of Baker on the way to the south and east entrance to Death Valley. They were developed during the late 1800's and operated intermittently depending on the price of the minerals.

For information concerning any specific aspect of this area, contact the Barstow Way Station, or District Manager of BLM, 1695 Spruce Street, Barstow, CA 92517 or (714) 787-1462.

GOLDSTONE (33 miles north of Barstow) was the site of extensive gold mining activity dating from 1881. Today NASA's Goldstone Deep Space Tracking Station is operated by the Jet Propulsion Laboratory of the California Institute of Technology. The tracking station is open to the public on a group tour basis only. Check with the station before planning a trip.

TOWN OF CALICO

CENTERED ABOUT THE "TOWN OF CALICO", THE CALICO MINING DISTRICT, WITH A PEAK POPULATION OF 3,000, PRODUCED $13-20 MILLION IN SILVER AND $9 MILLION IN BORATE MINERALS BETWEEN 1881-1907. ON APRIL 6, 1881, SEVERAL CLAIMS WERE LOCATED WHICH FORMED THE LARGEST MINE IN THE DISTRICT, THE SILVER KING. PROFITABLE MINING OF SILVER CEASED IN 1896.

Ernest Hommerd

The region lying southeast of the Rand Mountains is referred to as the High Desert country. Early mining activities produced a few mines that were worthwhile. The most noted among them were in the Calico Mountains just east of Barstow and the Goldstone Minine District north of there.

The CALICO GHOST TOWN (12 miles east of Barstow) had its beginnings in 1881, when the Silver King mine started the California Silver Rush. In two years active mines were scattered all over the Calico Hills. The peak years of productivity were 1884-1885. As a result of the decreased value of silver in 1886, mining dwindled until, by 1905 the town was deserted. During the 1900's mining operations came and went as the silver price fluctuated. The real silver mine now is not only the mining in the hills with the price of silver high, but the silver from tourists visiting the "ghost town".

When William Knott was a young man he worked in Calico. He saw the beauty and the value of the place so later, when he was able, bought and restored it. The original buildings of the town are long gone but new ones recreate the atmosphere and history of Calico's silver mining days.

It is now part of the San Bernardino County Park system and operated with mine train rides and other attractions. It is open to the public every day of the year except Christmas. Parking is available and overnight camping is at the Calico Campground just south of the Ghost Town.

Ernest Hommerd

Ernest Hommerding

"Seven miles north of Daggett is the much talked of city of Calico. One narrow and serpentine street is the only thoroughfare. The place is built on a narrow ledge, the back end of lots on each side of the street and on or over a bluff. Small, hastily-built houses are the order of buildings, only a few two-story houses gracing the camp. Saloons are more than numerous. Business generally is overdone, and the number of black-legs and tin-horn gamblers that infest the place is remarked by a newcomer. The only water supply is that hauled two miles from Evan's Well, and costs from 3 to 5 cents per gallon. Wood is $10 per cord. Board, $7 to $8 a week. The Occidental and Whitfield House are the only hotels, and they are pushed to their utmost capacity to accommodate the travel that is arriving daily. The camp is a good one, but at present is overestimated and over crowded by men out of money and work. Capital, development and a chance is all this camp needs to be a second edition to the Comstock at no great distant date."

from "Mining and Scientific Press, March 14, 1885"

Silver Mining in Old Calico by F. Harold Weber, Jr.

California Geology, May, 1966

A short twenty years later it was a ghost town! Some fifty mines of the Calico District—Silver King, Bismark, Waterman and Garfield, etc., produced approximately $20 million in silver—not the rich lode of the Comstock's $225 million as hoped for, but significant.

SOUTHWEST AREA
Lower Argus & Slate Ranges
Johannesburg - Trona - Ballarat
Lower Panamint Valley

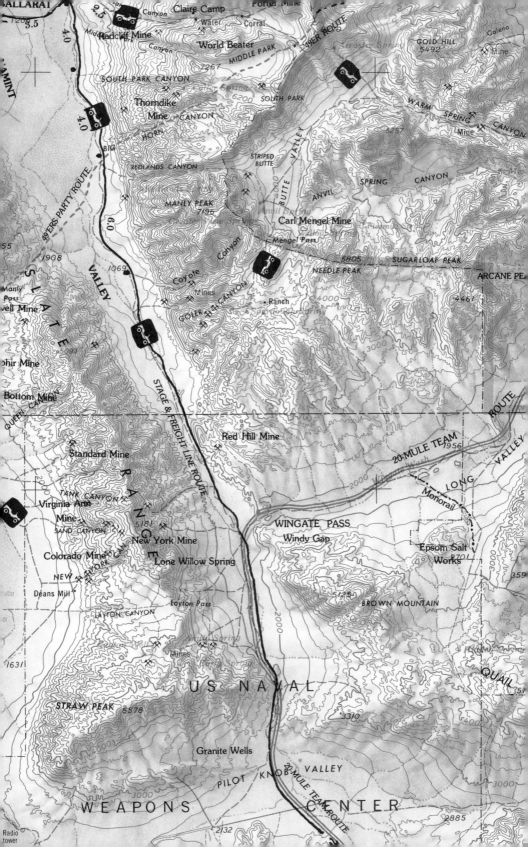

Trona
Pinnacles

Francile Hansen

SEARLES LAKE has the largest known saline deposits. It is the remains of one of the ancient lakes. Now it is a vast flat of mud and sand containing disseminated salt crystals averaging 71 feet in thickness and has an exposed area of twelve square miles. Surrounding the exposed body is a 20-square-mile area where commercial salts as much as 30 feet thick are covered with playa mud.

The production of salines at Searles Lake started about 1878 and over the years several companies have processed minerals here. Today the American Potash and Chemical Corporation has the principal operations producing potassium salts, borax, boric acid, bromine, lithium carbonate, and phosphoric acid. Much of these materials are in their pure form. Needing little processing at Trona, they are shipped by special railway cars directly to the outside refineries.

The American Trona Corporation was first formed in 1913. As production expanded and the chemicals we use are more numerous in our modern life of the space-jet age, the present city of Trona has developed into an active mining town. Three other company towns are situated along the ancient lakeshore—Westend, Borosolvay and Argus.

South of these four towns separating the flats of Searles Lake from its desert shores stand *THE PINNACLES*. Called Cathedral City by the old timers for its many shaped spires, these rough, porous formations were, in prehistoric times, underwater algae that developed when the land was lush and tropical. These multi-colored jasper-agate combination rocks have been picked over for years by rockhounds, yet small bits can still be found.

THE TANKS

Our stage and freight station was called The Tanks and was located on the old dirt road west of present day Valley Wells. It was a mid-way stop between Johannesburg and Skidoo. Water, stored in a large tank on a high platform, was secured via a small pipe laid on top of the ground to a spring near Indian Joe's place. It was the only reliable water between Trona and Panamint Valley. The Tanks was a repair and re-supply stop where mules were shod, feed was available for overnight stops, iron rims reset on wagon wheels and water barrels filled.

Indian Joe's Spring had been the home of Joe's family for as long as people could remember except for a time when some whites squatted there. They made a few improvements such as planting a few fruit trees before moving on. In the early 1900's when the Rinaldi and Clark freight lines operated, Joe with his sister and mother lived there. It was a marginal life at best with much of their time spent each day acquiring a survival diet. They gathered pinyon nuts up in the higher canyons and for meat had rabbits, small rodents and various reptiles they caught in traps. (Even the miners found the chuckawalla quite acceptable—if they could forget what he looked like.) In the summer they ate the figs, peaches and grapes but during the long winters, the food problem became quite critical for them. It was common practice for mine operators and freighters to carry extra dried or canned foods to help them.

About the only time we ever saw Joe was in mid-winter. At breakfast time we'd see him sitting on the back steps. Mother knew why. After the stage drivers and teamsters were fed, she'd make up a sack of food and set it out with a friendly word. No response other than a slight nod and he'd be on his way home.

One trip when Dad was about to pull out for Johannesburg, he found Joe sitting by the wagons away from the shops. This was unusual. He told Dad that the Trona people were going to take his spring. With some inquiry, Dad found out that a surveyor had been planning on running a line from Trona to the spring to get more drinking water, without the permission from Joe or regard for his family.

Without comment, Dad went over and picked up the mailbag and started to pull his team out. The Trona company man hailed him down and wanted to know why he didn't pick up the freight to go. Dad answered, "I don't want to haul for anybody that would steal from an Indian."

A company man had to come out all the way from Los Angeles to reassure Dad that Joe and his family could stay at the springs as long as they wanted to. It was easier to find other water than it was to get another teamster to haul their freight. Deep-well drilling farther out on the flats produced a good supply of water for the town of Trona—it is now called Valley Wells.

JOHANNESBURG—SKIDOO
Stage and Freight Line

RINALDI & CLARK FREIGHTING

At first burros and mule pack trains served the miners and prospectors needs. As demands grew, four to six-horse stages carried passengers and mail, with large long-line outfits hauling the freight. The Panamint mines were supplied with primitive roads that ran along the eastern side of the Valley and across the high desert to Barstow and San Bernardino. As mines were discovered and worked, and towns developed, supplies and mail demanded more efficient transportation. Railway spurs were built and in the late 1800's railroad lines were extended from Kramer to Johannesburg, also to Garlock, and to the mines east of Death Valley north of Las Vegas. Freighting then was done between numerous sidings and the mines.

In winter and summer stage coaches and freight teams left almost daily from the Johannesburg Railway and Stage Station for the mines in the Slate, Argus, and Panamint ranges. Roads were still little more than wheel tracks in the deep sand or narrow cuts on the mountain slopes. Water was scarce between Stage Stations especially for so many animals. Water barrels were mounted on each side of most wagons. An assistant (swamper) rode with the teamster and helped carry water in buckets to the thirsty horses and mules at their frequent rest stops.

Most of the Rinaldi & Clark outfits were made up of two big wagons and a feed wagon pulled by twelve to eighteen head. Although mules held up better in the intense heat, my father preferred horses and estimated his loads and schedules accordingly. It was a seventeen day round trip between Joburg and Skidoo (some 85 miles). Except for a few places like The Tanks or Wildrose where feed could be stockpiled, teamsters carried their hay with them and fed in the feed wagon at night.

Hardships of many kinds became routine experiences. In summer the furnace-heat of the ground temperatures in the flat salt basins and the winter's sleet-laden winds across the Slate Range and Harrisburg Flat were vicious challenges to man and beast. At times summer dust clouds, or winter's driving snow made it impossible to see the leaders of the team. In the canyons, summer cloudbursts could wipe out roads and sometimes stock and wagons. The Slate Range crossing was an experience that tested the skills of the best teamster. On the south side it was a very steep, narrow track between huge rocks. At the summit, where the highway now crosses, is a small flat area which was used for passing or regrouping the wagons and stock.

I'll always remember the last trip I took with Dad over to Ballarat. It had been a long, hot pull from The Tanks requiring many "breathers" for the horses and a lot of water buckets packed before we reached Big Flat at the south foot of the range. It was late afternoon. I figured we were all ready to make camp. However, Dad began unhooking the heavy lead wagon from the rest of the outfit and soon we were on the way again up to the summit. It took all the power of the big team to haul it to the top. Dad locked the wheels and we left it. The team was then taken back down to the Big Flat camp. By then, it was quite dark. A kerosene lantern provided light to tie up the stock to the feed wagon and distribute all the grain and hay. You'll never know how much tired, thirsty horses can drink unless you were tired and had to pack water to sixteen head after they had put in a long day of hauling.

A stiff desert wind was blowing as we prepared supper over a sage-stump fire. Cooking utensils consisted of three items—a blackened coffee pot, a big frypan for the bacon, and a pot in which to boil some potatoes. Behind a barrier of baled hay we did real well by staying out of the cold wind until a sudden gust blew some loose sage into the frypan. "Seasoning" was all my dad said, as he poured bacon and sage gravy over the spuds.

It seemed I had just gotten to sleep when the horses began moving around a lot. Then I heard my dad holler, "Build a fire under the coffee while I finish hooking up." Oh, boy, morning already! It seemed like the middle of the night. However it was daylight by the time we got under way to pull the second wagon along with the feed wagon to the top of the pass. By mid-morning we had the whole outfit together again ready to go down the grade into Panamint Valley.

Then began the real test of a teamster's skill—to get the entire outfit down the steep, winding grade without the wagons piling up on the teams or sliding over the rocky side. The heavy wagons were rolled forward onto great iron shoes so the rear wheels and brakes were locked. Like giant sleds, they were gingerly skidded down the steep, twisting road and around hairpin turns until the bottom flats were reached and the wheel-shoes were removed.

My dad's horses were trained to perform specific jobs. The *leaders* were the most intelligent and experienced because they had to set the pace for the string behind them. The *swing team*, between four or eight horses depending on the load Dad was hauling, were the workers who did not require much training. They just needed to know their names and when to "whoa" or "pull". The *pointers, sixes,* and *eights* were trained to respond to commands by name. They had to step over the middle hookup chain to pull in the opposite direction on the turns. They kept the wagons moving forward instead of cramping into the bank or going over the cliff. After the turn was made they stepped back into place to straighten out the line. *Wheelers* were the strongest and largest, also experienced, who were nearly always horses even if a teamster used mules for the main team. They kept the load moving forward on turns.

46   Ballarat Stage   Billy Clark's Grandchildren

When my dad had a light freight haul he preferred his special horses which he could ride up on the seat of the wagon and control his team with only hand reins and the spoken command. On big heavy loads where more than twelve animals were needed, he rode the nigh (left) wheeler. From this position he could manage the team and the wagons by working the brakes or the brake rope and the jerkline. The brakes on the wagon had a long handle Dad could operate with his foot or pull on the rope. The jerkline was a rope going through the rings on the left side of the harness of each animal and was attached to the nigh (left) leaders bit.

To turn the team to the left, a steady pull on the jerkline of the nigh leader would direct the leaders to the left. The "off" (right) leader would follow as he was attached to the nigh leader by a strap fastened to his collar. To turn to the right, a series of short, sharp jerks on the line signaled the nigh leader to swing right, which would automatically alert the off leader to swing to the right also. Turning this long-line outfit was tricky business. It required communication and understanding between the drivers and their team. The term "muleskinner" originally grew out by the practice of some drivers who "roughed up" their team. Good drivers were usually soft-spoken and skillful in their handling of the outfit without abusing his stock.

Bells were fastened to the collars of the lead animals to alert other teamsters that another team was coming. On this trip with my Dad we met no other outfit. The team going downhill usually pulled over the first available pullout to let the team pass that was coming uphill. This gave the driver a chance to keep his momentum up as it was hard in the narrow canyons and on grades to roll again if they had to stop. Bells were not used on open country as the great clouds of dust would signal an approach of a team many miles away. Smaller sets of bells were used on stage coaches— each bell was of a different size to produce a matched tone or chord which became an identifiable sound personal to each teamster. All the other teamsters could recognize bell tones and would know who was coming, even though they might not be able to see them.

By now it was getting late in the day, so the camp at the bottom of the grade on the north side of the Slate Range looked good. It would give the team plenty of time to eat and rest before crossing the desolate Panamint flat to Ballarat. However, a recent cloudburst had washed out some of the road there. Work had to be done on the road before my dad could take his big wagons across it. From the looks of the brush hung up on the walls of the wash, the flood must have been better than twenty feet deep as it swept through. It had flooded part of the road across the salt flats too, making it unsafe for the big load. We had to take the long haul up the west side of the valley and around the north end of the soft lakebed. The muggy heat was intense and only short pulls at a time could be made before resting the horses. I was really kept busy packing buckets of water at each rest stop. Upon our arrival at Ballarat there was no rest at first. The freight had to be unloaded for the nearby mines and hay had to be unloaded for the stock.

47

PANAMINT VALLEY

The first unwitting white visitors were the Jayhawkers and perhaps some of the Bennett-Arcane Party. In 1849 these pioneers lost their way and separated in Death Valley when escaping on an "every man for himself" basis. A year later it is recorded that members of a US Geological Survey Team camped at a spring near the present site of Ballarat on their reconnaissance of the Panamints. These early visitors related many versions of their experiences but in a few things they agreed. It was a miserable place! Yet, treasures were sure to be found somewhere in these desolate hills. One originated the legend of finding a chunk of pure silver on his way through from the north and using it for a sight on his rifle. As near as it (the "Lost Gunsight" mine) could be reconstructed, the place where the ore was supposedly picked up by one of the "Mississippi Boys" was along the wash near present day Stovepipe Wells. No other trace of such ore has ever been found there.

Panamint City was the substantial start of Ballarat. Early in 1873 a Wells Fargo bullion shipment was robbed to the west of Panamint Valley. The robbers hid out in steep, narrow, Surprise Canyon to the east in the Panamint Range. This rough, remote canyon was a great place to hide When whiling away their time waiting for the heat of their robbery to cool, one of the men discovered a ledge of pure silver that promised far more return than what the robbery had netted them. One of the robbers knew of Senator Stewart of Nevada. Stewart became the intermediary who arranged a deal in which they would return all their stolen loot in exchange for immunity from the law. Senator Stewart's price for his help was a piece of the mine action. Subsequently claims were filed and the Panamint Mining District was organized. News of the silver strike quickly spread and soon scores of prospectors swarmed up the torturous canyon. To supply them, freighters and stages began operating between Panamint Valley and San Bernardino. Remi Nadeau was the freighter and at one time, to protect his load against robbery, he transported silver bullion in 750 pound balls.

Panamint City (elevation 7500') was nine miles up the canyon. The road was little more than wheel tracks through brush and around huge rocks. The town started as a handful of shanty structures strung out for

48

more than a mile on each side of the narrow valley. It was so steep and narrow there was no room for a second street. It developed into a rough town of 5000 people with saloons, stores, and board shanties to house them. The isolation encouraged violence where guns settled arguments without any assistance from lawyers or courts. Result—some fifty to sixty men were killed in its short life. Production reached its height in 1874-1875 with over 700 men working the mine. Within four years the rich silver deposit faded. In 1876, to add to the decision to move out, a great flash flood roared down the canyon destroying many of the buildings. By 1878 another "boom" was over for those who had come to "pan-a-mint of gold from them thar hills."

As the mine began declining, the prospectors moved over to the Darwin area where rich silver ore was found. The Modoc Mine, started in 1875, brought new hope to the area. This mine has been referred to as the Hearst Mine. George Hearst, father of William Randolph, was reported to have been the owner. The main period of operation was up to 1890 with an initial $1,900,000 gross production. Since that time by reworking the slag and dumps some $450,000 was taken out. The ore was a complex of gold, silver, lead, copper, and zinc.

Few metals are usable in their pure form except gold. To separate the ore from the unwanted elements it was necessary to reduce the silver to a melted state, then poured into bars for transport. This process of smelting needed extensive heat. Since coal was not in the area, the only source of fuel near the Modoc Mine was the pinyon forest across the Valley up in Wildrose Canyon. Burning the wood into charcoal in the beehive shaped kilns provided the necessary heating fuel for the smelters.

The community serving the Modock Consolidated Mining Company and the Minnietta Mine just south of it was Lookout. This well-equipped company town was perched on top of Lookout Mountain. Today it can be visited via the jeep road marked "Minnietta Mine" off Hwy. 190 or by following the Panamint Springs road north out of Trona. Parts of the road around the old mines in this area are steep and rough where a 4x4 drive is necessary.

The road built by Remi Nadeau, the teamster servicing the Modock and Minnietta Mines, was so straight it was called his "shotgun road". It was the first in the desert to be surveyed. From the summit of the Slate Range, you can see it today going straight north up the west side of the Panamint Valley.

Lookout   Courtesy of Maturango Museum

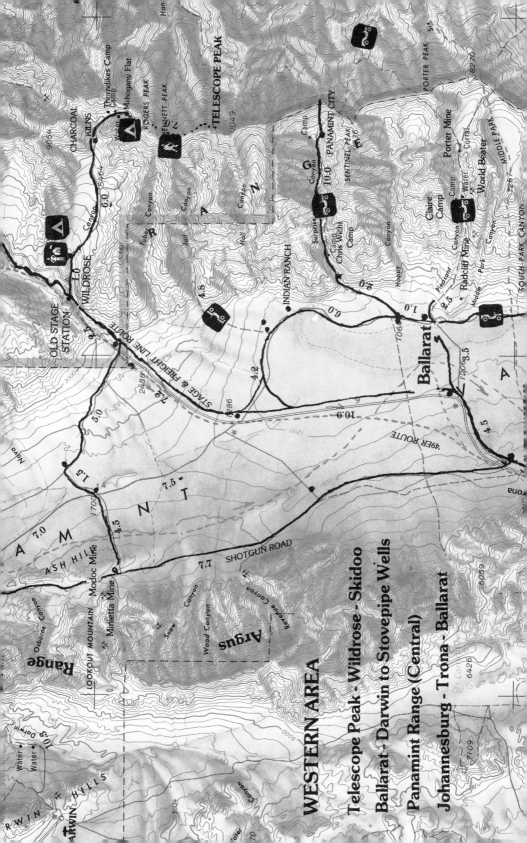

WESTERN AREA

Telescope Peak - Wildrose - Skidoo

Ballarat - Darwin to Stovepipe Wells

Panamint Range (Central)

Johannesburg - Trona - Ballarat

BALLARAT —A WAY STATION TO SOMEWHERE ELSE

Appropriately named after the gold center half a world away in Australia, it might well have been called Turnstile. It had so little to offer except as a temporary meeting place for those on their way up or down the long valley to some place else. It started as a way station for prospectors, miners, teamsters, and speculators. Even the Indians who lived at nearby Indian Ranch spent most of the long summers in higher valleys where the pine nuts and game were more plentiful. In its setting at the eastern edge of the crusted salt beds of Panamint Valley, the weather is intolerable. In winter the downdrafts from the snow covered Panamints are freezing. In summer the oppressive heat hovers as high as 112° at two o'clock in the morning. Its excuse for existence lay in its location. A meeting place for those living some other place.

Before the "Silver Stampede" of the Modoc and Minnietta ceased all operations, gold was discovered across the Valley up in Pleasant Canyon. Ballarat became a city for the workers of Ratcliff Mine, located a short distance up the canyons. The most prosperous years of the Ratcliff was from 1898 to 1903. With over 200 men working the mine in a narrow, steep canyon, the only place for a town was down on the flats below.

Organized in 1897, Ballarat soon developed into an active town of some 500 residents. Its business district included the Calloway Hotel, a stage and Wells Fargo station, almost a dozen saloons, and two stores. For a time it was the seat of government for southern Inyo County with its own Justice of the Peace. By 1899 a one-room school was built as well as a jail.

The Teagle Brothers of Johannesburg established a store in 1900. They also had a rooming house and a feed and supply yard for the freight teams. The invention of the swamp cooler "air conditioner" made the rooms at the hotel a premium. From the eaves of the building burlap were hung with water slowly dripping down onto it from pipes that were installed around the building. As the wind blew and the air evaporated, coolness penetrated throughout the rooming house.

In 1905 the Ratcliff Mine closed. Its rich ore had been worked by crude methods. Then, between 1927 and 1940, more than $250,000 was secured by reworking the tailings from the old mill. Other mines in the Pleasant Canyon region were the Gold Bug, the O.B. Joyful, Porter, The Gem, Matchless, and the World Beater.

As mines developed in the Panamints, Ballarat became a supply center for both sides of the Valley. The Wells Fargo Office and Stage Station was owned and operated by Rinaldi and Clark.

When the mines played out and their workers moved on to other diggings, the need for Ballarat was gone. The arrival of cars, trucks, and hard surfaced roads brought in a new era to mining.

Ballarat is no more. The town was declared a State Historical Site and dedicated December 3, 1949 by Representatives of the State Historical Society and the Death Valley 49'ers organization. Today it is in a sad state. In the past twenty-five years little concern has been shown for its care. Winds and rain have torn off the roofs and eroded the soft clay-brick walls of the houses. What the weather didn't do the souvenir hunters and deliberate vandalism have finished. Two or three old buildings and some partial walls are left. The only activity is that of a repair equipment outfit that has a number of old cars, trucks, and mining junk that is being cannibalized to service a few casual or weekend miners in the canyons nearby. The true and faithful residents of the valley have been the antelope ground squirrels and lizards. A few Indians still live at Indian Ranch in Hall Canyon.

Perhaps that is as it should be—all revert back to the original state. The old prospectors and miners moved out except those who went into the steep canyons and were never heard from again. Or, those like the old stage driver "Slim", who can be found just west of town in what's left of the old cemetery.

BALLARAT DAZE or SHORTY'S FIRST FUNERAL

The Fourth of July was a "Hooraw" time for sure, in Ballarat. Miners, prospectors and teamsters and businessmen joined to celebrate the day in great style—in fact, it usually lasted several days. It was about the third day of such a celebration when things had slowed down and everything was getting a bit dull that one of the boys observed, "You know, Shorty's been under the bottle pretty near a week now. Let's sober him up some so he can enjoy himself a bit before he goes back to his camp."

Chris Wicht's was the only saloon with a pool table. On it was placed a hastely built coffin-like box. Shorty, well under the influence, was wrapped from head to foot in an old white sheet so only his face would show. He was carefully lowered into the box and placed on top of the pool table. Candles were spread all around it and he was left to finish his "nap".

About dark, Shorty began to stir a bit. Chris Wicht sent word down the street that Shorty was coming around. Soon the men began arriving from all over town. Some of the men had not been taken in on the scheme so they thought at first it was the real thing. They all gathered around Shorty. The candles were lit. And they all watched while Shorty opened his eyes. He lay there, fully awake, taking in everything, including such remarks as, "What a nice guy he had been" and "Hope he's found his gold mine up there somewhere." It was when they blew out the candles and picked up the coffin to pack it out to the cemetery, that Shorty began yelling.

. . . It was quite some time before he showed up in Ballarat again. I'm sure it was much longer before Shorty got over his Fourth of July funeral at Ballarat.

WILDROSE CANYON

Panamints from Slate Range

Wildrose Canyon, named by the miners because of the many wild roses that grew near the springs, has witnessed the coming and going of men and wildlife since pre-whiteman times. First the Indians, then the pioneers, prospectors and freighters. Once this narrow canyon was a continuous scene of activity as freight outfits took their turn negotiating the difficult grades and switchbacks with supplies, charcoal, ore and heavy mining equipment. In the 1930's and 40's some gold had been recovered from placer and lode deposits in the area. The three most active lode gold mines were the Burro, Gem and New Discovery. The placer mining was small and inconsequential.

Freight lines carrying supplies destined for Skidoo usually by-passed Ballarat and followed along much the same route as the present highway. In wet periods, when rains softened the short cut across the old lakebed, freighters to Ballarat also kept to the west—going around the lake and coming in from the north.

The route between Panamint Valley to Skidoo was a long, hot, tough climb up deep washes and around short treacherous turns. Today's visitor can well imagine the skill needed in handling stock and equipment to make such a trip. The driver sitting on his high seat of the lead wagon had from six to ten pairs of mules ahead and two freight wagons and a feed wagon behind him. Some turns were so sharp half of the team was out of sight around a bend before the first wagon reached the turn.

In summer it was a tedious, hot drag between the Water Canyon camp at the foot of the Slate Range and Wildrose Spring. In the oppressive heat, stops had to be made so the driver and his swamper could carry buckets of water from the great wooden barrels attached to each side of the wagons to the exhausted animals.

When extra heavy loads were being hauled, camp would be made on the north edge of the lakebed at Cheesebrough's Spring. The next day would be spent hauling one wagon at a time up the wash to Wildrose Station—a shuttle operation that took all day. At Wildrose there was a good camp off the road near a high overhanging cliff. The campfire-smoked cliff can still be seen where countless freighters and prospectors blackened the high walls.

55

Stock was fed in a long feed wagon and they were watered at the running spring. Supper was a simple affair cooked between a couple of rocks in a pot or two, or a frypan and a "billy can" for the black coffee. The bedroll was of great proportion as the desert nights in the high canyons got really cold. With a dog curled up at the foot of the bed and the fire low, yarns were swapped about other times, people, and experiences.

On one of the nights we camped there we heard thunder in the mountains up on Telescope. Dad was really nervous about that for awhile. He went to bed with all his clothes on and boots handy, just in case. The rumbling drifted on and everything quieted down. Then Dad recalled:

"Several years ago, Earl Coffee and I camped here together. In the middle of the night a thunderstorm struck the upper canyons. It was really big. Lightning all over the sky. No rumblings that night, just great crashing booms. We knew what that meant. Untying all the stock we whopped them up the canyon to a higher bench just in time. Water came tumbling and roaring down this canyon as we'd never seen before or since. Sand and rock were rolling. An undercut bank collapsed, turning the main force of the stream against our camp. The big lead wagon loaded with supplies for Skidoo was lifted and shoved over against the canyon wall. The second wagon loaded with the new heavy machinery and the feed wagon went rolling down the canyon. We were lucky to get out when we did or we would have lost all our stock.

The next morning we found the lead wagon all okay, half buried in sand and gravel. The feed wagon was light and rode the flood all the way down canyon to the cutoff road to Ballarat. The other wagon with the heavy machinery was nowhere in sight. Loaded with such heavy freight it probably rolled into a deep gulch somewhere and then was buried by the flood. That wagon was never found! It was a brand new Studebaker wagon I had just bought!"

56

Ed Rivers was our Wildrose Station Manager, helping with stage stock and occasionally accommodating an overnight guest, if he had his own bedroll. On the side, he raised goats to sell for meat to the miners. Wouldn't touch the stuff himself. There were hundreds of them scattered in the nearby hills and up on Harrisburg flat. One night when we camped by the spring a herd of them moved in on the Station. Goats everywhere! The young ones were all over the feed cart, walking the rail fencing, and even up on the roof of Ed's cabin. Dad wasn't too pleased about the smelly critters "stinking up the place where his prize team of horses had to be watered." But, it only happened now and then when the herd moved down for a drink.

Charcoal Kilns - Wildrose   NPS Photo

Just beyond the upper Wildrose Spring a road continues east to the head of the canyon. There is a Park Ranger Station a short half mile from the junction. Before air conditioning the summer headquarters of the Park Service was located here. A Ranger is now on duty there to give assistance and information.

Above the Ranger Station about seven miles, are ten Charcoal Kilns. Built back in the 1870's to provide charcoal for the Modock Mine, these kilns are thirty feet across. They were constructed by Chinese laborers from a Swiss engineer's design. These great stone ovens are still in good condition—a testimony to their workmanship—and their protection under Park Service supervision. Indians were paid to cut the pinyon trees and prepare the wood for the burning. After firing, the resulting charcoal was packed on mules and transported across the Panamint Valley to the Modock smelters up on Lookout Mountains.

The dirt road leading to the upper end of the canyon gets very steep and rough. It is not advisable for heavy cars or RV's. Winter snows lay until late spring. Check with the Ranger on road conditions before starting this trip.

MAHOGANY FLAT (8133') is at the end of the road. There is a small campground and picnic site but no water there. Long ago Indians gathered large quantities of pinyon nuts in this forested area.

Telescope Peak

Rocky Rockwell

PANAMINT SUMMIT TRAILS

TELESCOPE PEAK TRAIL (7.0 miles—6-8 hours round trip). The trail to the peak starts at Mahogany Flats. Late spring (May-June) and early fall (September-October) are the best times to make the ascent. In winter it is snowcapped and dangerous. In mid-summer it can be quite hot in open, exposed places. It is recommended as acceptable to climb for anyone in reasonably good physical condition. Carry your water as there is none on the trail. Check with the Ranger about trail and weather conditions.

TELESCOPE PEAK (11,049') is the highest peak in this part of the Basin Ranges. It was named by W. T. Henderson, the first man to scale it in 1860. From its summit is a 360 degree view of great magnitude: east, across Death Valley to the Amargosa Desert, beyond the Black and Greenwater mountains to the Charleston peaks north of Las Vegas, south, to the Owlshead and Avawitz mountains; north to the Last Chance Range, and the Funeral and Grapevine mountains; and west, across the Panamint Basin and Inyo Mountains to the Sierra Nevada. It is a unique viewpoint where "high mountains and deep valleys" can be seen at their best. Telescope Peak is on the crest of the Panamint fault. From its summit this east facing front drops more than 11,000' to the existing floor of Death Valley. Drilling tests show it continues downward under the surface more than a mile!

WILDROSE PEAK (9064')

For the ambitious hiker there are several other peaks near Telescope, all above 9000 feet. A less extensive hike would be to Wildrose Peak. The trailhead is at the west end of the Charcoal Kilns (6800'). This four-mile trip takes about four to six hours for the round trip. The trail is not too difficult and affords many outlooks to the east over Death Valley and west over Panamint Valley. Be sure to take a snack, water, and film. From Wildrose Peak a trail continues north along the high summit of the range to a junction with the Auguereberry Point-Trail Canyon jeep road.

There is quite a range of plant and animal life on this trip. In one day the extreme from playa floor to mountain crest can be encountered. Above the Charcoal Kilns most of the slopes are covered with pinyon and limber pines, some juniper, and on the higher slopes can be seen the ancient bristlecone pines.

58

Amply supplied with water from a number of springs, it has provided shelter and food to a wide variety of birds and animals ranging from hummingbirds to mountain sheep. In recent years the offsprings from the prospectors' old faithful burro left in the desert has become a real problem of growing magnitude. Today more than 1600 ferril burros live in Death Valley Monument. Most of them are in this northern Panamint region.

They have no natural predators, therefore they increase at an alarming rate. The damage to the environment has become more and more evident in recent years. For instance, the overgrazing in many places has been to the detriment of a large number of smaller animals and plants upon which they feed. The desert bighorns are being crowded out by these animals introduced by man. As the Park Service has summarized: "The Monument cannot operate as a natural area and a burro sanctuary since the two concepts are ecologically incompatible."

Many efforts have been made to resolve the situation, all of them inadequate. Burros have been sandwiched in as part of Death Valley's "wildlife" which is sheer nonsense. If there were an overpopulation of rattlesnakes or bobcats crawling through the campgrounds biting our dogs and children, there would be plenty of public support to reduce the snake and bobcat population. Trying to reduce the burro population has become a real headache to the administration of the Monument.

The "free burro" concept merely sweeps the problem under the rug for the moment while the area of their destruction expands. Today's understandings of environmental impact should never sanction such acceptance. It is interesting to observe that those most vocal to "save the wild burros" are usually the people farthest removed from the area and least responsible for the survival of our great desert ecology.

HARRISBURG

Whenever there was excitement or a "Hooraw" going on, Shorty Harris was sure to be there. He had a sense of timing about what was about to happen and would show up at the most unexpected places and times. He was a true Rainbow Chaser who spent his life looking for the pot of gold. He found it several times, but soon sold out to others to do the development and get the big money. He celebrated by giving it all away to someone he wanted to help; for drinks on the house to his pals; or get taken in a stock swindle assessment with only worthless paper to show for his discovery. It was easy-come, easy-go with Shorty as long as the boys could swap yarns with him, buy a drink and share a good joke. He was a kindly, uncomplicated person who loved to talk and drink at Chris Wicht's saloon in Ballarat. It always wound up as his home base for his wanderings. Someone was always around who had been on the hunt too. If he ever had a place he called home it was probably there.

Shorty was a well built man—except that his legs were too short for the rest of him. He was in good shape, only too short. His pants were too long, his coat was too long and its sleeves were too long. His flappy old hat and a large mustache covered most of his face. However, after talking to him at close range you always remembered his friendly eyes and gold-capped front teeth.

Once, when things had been getting slow in Rhyolite he headed out across Death Valley and over the Panamints to join in the usual celebration that was sure to be held in Ballarat on the Fourth of July. Along the way he talked another prospector, Pete Auguereberry into going along with him. They stopped for the night on the big flat just south of Skidoo. Here the story varies according to whether you hear Shorty's or Pete's account. At any rate, a discovery was made there that summer morning in 1906. They went on down into Ballarat to spread the news, then returned to stake their claim along with quite a few other Ballarat boys. Several had gotten there

60

ahead of Shorty and Pete and staked the claims for themselves. Pete assured them that he and Shorty had found it. The claimjumpers pulled up their stakes and moved out.

Almost within hours a camp was born that was to become a town. Pete, a quiet man of Basque descent, worked while Shorty talked. It was inevitable that the town, that soon grew to several hundred people, was called Harrisburg. Most of the buildings were only tents with wood floors and sides. It was soon evident that the big strike might be only a limited outcropping. Within a few days of Shorty's and Pete's discovery a couple of fellows found rich ore just over the north hill. Harrisburg soon faded. All that was left of Shorty's town was the brush covered flat around it. The camp was stripped of its tents and lumber to be reassembled at Skidoo. Mining and building materials were precious in this land so far away from the railroad and they were all moved to new diggings along with the owners.

Shorty sold his interest in the mine early but it wasn't until much later a developer came around and Pete sold. This large outfit worked it for years before it played out. Later, after they left Pete returned to the mine and worked it for many years as a one-man operation. He didn't have the richest mine in the Panamints but what he made was his and he was his own boss. He enjoyed the desert and on the ridge to the east he did have the greatest view in the Panamints of the entire Death Valley region. He was so proud of it he brushed out a road up to a high point that was later, very fittingly given the name Augereberry Point.

To enjoy his favorite view, take the short trail from the present parking area. This breathtaking colorama expands from Badwater north to the Daylight Pass country. The jeep road to Death Valley from Auguereberry Point via Trail Canyon drops some 2500' with steep grades and sharp switchbacks. It could be washed out in places. Check with the Ranger Station before making this trip.

Pete Auguereberry at his Mine

Shorty often stopped at our stage and blacksmith shop at The Tanks, near Trona, on his way "outside" or heading back to the Panamints. Overnight was as long as he would stay and he slept out with his burros by the blacksmith shop. He appreciated a little hay for his pets, a new strap for a pack saddle, and especially a home cooked meal by my mother who cooked for the teamsters and drummers on their way to the mines.

The last time we ever saw Shorty was some years later, in Fresno, when the Raisin Day Parade was followed in the afternoon by an automobile race on the big dirt track. And, true to form, there was Shorty whooping it up on the top of an "Old Timers" float in the parade. His vocabulary hadn't lost any of its color and his excitement in seeing us was almost his undoing as he nearly fell off the wagon.

I never heard about Shorty again until some twenty years later when I went to Death Valley to work as a Naturalist for the Park Service. Shorty was there. He had died in Big Pine, November 10, 1934 and requested that in his last great Hooraw he be buried alongside of his old friend Jim Dayton.

SKIDOO (1905-1917 - Reworked in the 1930's)

The northern Panamints had been by-passed for decades, first by the 49er's who had lost their way, then by the burro prospectors on their way to other places. With the great boom in the Bullfrog-Rhyolite area to the east and the development of numerous mines in the vicinity of Ballarat, at first large numbers of prospectors and miners invaded the region. Then, as the operations were reduced and the few well paying mines were bought up by large capital interests, the little fellows moved on.

It was no accident that gold was discovered on the high shoulder of Tucki Mountain. Prospectors were looking everywhere. A few days after Shorty's and Pete's discovery at Harrisburg, a couple of tenderfoot prospectors, with beginner's luck, found gold in the little canyon just north of there. They soon sold out for $60 thousand to Bob Montgomery of Rhyolite, and Skidoo was born. In the early days of desert mining successful gold operations have always been dependent upon a good supply of water nearby to make a mine pay. It was necessary to process the ore as well as for the needs of the workers. There was little water on the crest of Tucki. Bob Montgomery, in his usual flamboyant style, had freighters (including Rinaldi and Clark) haul in enough 6" cast iron pipe from Johannesburg to carry water from a large spring on the shoulders of Telescope Peak to the mine—some 23 miles of it. The slang expression "23-Skidoo to you" was soon applied to the community at the end of the long pipeline.

Recent reports of the Bureau of Mines indicate that "the area is underlain by quarts monzonite and other granite rocks. Ore deposits consist of a number of north and northest striking quartz veins that contain free gold—only a few feet thick." A number of high grade pockets have been found there. Principal mines in the Skidoo District were: Del Norte, Emigrant Springs, McBride, Napoleon, Sunset, Treasure Hill, Tucki, and Skidoo—which produced more than $1.5 million in gold.

Skidoo was operated primarily as a one-man company town. The usual early arrivals conducted themselves typical of rough and ready camps, but with the development of the mine, they soon moved on. Wildbunch stories (true or not) have been associated with all mining towns. Actually, Skidoo and Johannesburg had records of being almost too peaceful to be interesting. With stages, organized freight lines and railroads came lumber to build houses, more varied supplies, and most influential, family groups. My sister lived in Skidoo for some time in a plank floor and wall-tent while her husband worked at the mill. Actually, with a good wood/coal cookstove, they and their babies were quite comfortable. They even planted grain around the front to have a little green patch. In warm weather food items were placed in large clay pots. It was wrapped in damp burlap sacking and the evaporation kept the food in good condition. For social life the families joined in a neighbor atmosphere for pot luck suppers, box socials, or songfests.

The number of instances of disorder or violence in the prime days of the Skidoo operation would, actually, sum up about as favorable as most small communities today. For some time my oldest brother in his early teens, drove a four-horse stage between Skidoo and Johannesburg via Ballarat. Carrying mail, Wells Fargo express and passengers he had no serious difficulties. The frequent shipment of gold bullion was wrapped in a grain sack and stuffed under the driver's seat. He never realized how dangerous it was until, after we left the desert and got to watching western movies. The story of Skidoo's hanging, retold in several versions according to who was listening, was typical of the times.

Skidoo Digging

There's not much left of old Skidoo. When the ore ran out so did the need to stay. The twenty-three miles of pipe was dismantled and hauled out for scrap during World War I. Anything useful was hauled away to other camps. A few years ago some visitors were seen leaving the area in a great hurry. Soon, thereafter a tall cloud of black smoke indicated the end of another relic of the west's great mining days. About all that can be found now are a few empty holes, a burned out mill site, and a few old rusty cans and broken bottles. Here and there are a few rock and cement rectangles marking the places that supported the tent houses and buildings—and, a forlorn cemetery where the desert winds and grave-robber relic hunters have carried away everything movable into obscurity.

Skidoo Mill

EMIGRANT CANYON

This deep, narrow canyon provided a welcome respite from Death Valley to some of the weary '49ers where they found shade, cold springs, and a promise of higher ground and escape. Some fifty years later prospectors and miners rested here before making the daybreak crossing of Death Valley to Rhyolite. Some, such as Val Nolan, didn't make it.

During the days of Skidoo, a telephone line ran down Telephone Canyon, down Emigrant Wash, across the valley, over Daylight Pass to the Bullfrog-Rhyolite mines. Although evidence of poles and wires have long ago disappeared, its route and the wagon-track trail that followed it can still be seen. Looking across the valley from west of Stovepipe Wells Village the bare, shrubless pathway runs straight across the desert floor towards Death Valley Buttes. Plant life has not reclaimed the route even after seventy-five years!

65

STOVEPIPE WELLS VILLAGE

Historically this western gateway of Death Valley has witnessed the passing of primitive people, lost '49ers, prospectors and miners. Today's year-round vacationers will find accommodations including full hotel services, pool, store, service station, campgrounds and trailer park with activities of evening Park Naturalist programs and daytime field trips.

The original old Stovepipe Well is out in the Sand Dune area. It was a very shallow affair. With an old section of stovepipe used to keep it open, early day prospectors were grateful for a drink there.

MOSAIC & GROTTO CANYONS nearby provide unusual desert trips. Short, well-graded dirt roads lead to each. Allow about a half-day for each canyon. The short but violent thunderstorms which occur during the summer are largely responsible for the rock-fragment cover that has greatly modified the appearance of the desert basin. Sand, gravel, and boulders, washed in raging torrents from slopes at the wide upper ends of canyons, are funneled through deep, constricted gorges. As the debris-laden water breaks out of the confines of these "hourglass" canyons, it spreads out, loses speed, and abruptly deposits the rock debris (alluvium) in the shape of fans.

SAND DUNE AREA

The sand of the great dunes in the central part of the valley was brought there by winds from the west and south. Passing around Tucki Mountain the winds lost their velocity and carrying-power allowing the fine grains to settle on the old lakebed. Quartz, which largely forms the sand, originated in granite bedrock now exposed in various places throughout the monument. Flowing water has carried the weathered granite particles from the mountains and spread them out on alluvial fans. As the softer material eroded away, the resitant quartz, left exposed to the wind, was reduced to sand particles and then blown into piles that eventually became large dunes. With every wind, the contour of the dunes changes and the footprints of man and animals are erased. Winds deflected by mountain ridges blow the sand in one direction, then another, trapping the dunes where they stand.

Moisture runoff from adjacent mountains provided considerable water for the numerous springs in the area enabling the continuous flow of Salt Creek. Indians spent much of their winter time in or near these dunes where they found shelter, fuel, and food from the mesquite trees.

Although they seem quite barren they support an interesting wildlife community. The extensive number of grasses and mesquite trees indicate ample moisture close to the surface. Go into the dunes at daybreak before winds wipe out the many varied trails of visitors who shun the sun and hot sand by day but become quite active at night—kangaroo rats, beetles, lizards, coyotes, bobcats, sidewinder rattlers, and the ubiquitous kit fox that evidences good hunting there.

Visitors today will find the dunes rich in colorful photographic scenes in early morning or sunset hours. At the first indication of a wind storm, do not tarry. Within a few minutes it can become quite disagreeable, even dangerous. The day-use area provides a close-up entry to the larger dunes. A good dirt road leads to the picnic area and parking. There is no water here. Bring your own.

NPS Photo

BACKCOUNTRY TRIPS

Ventures into the Cottonwood Mountain canyons require a 4x4 drive. It is a remote, seldom visited place and extra concern should be made about selecting equipment and advising others of your plans. The route to Lemoigne Canyon takes off across Emigrant Wash about 6.0 miles west of Stovepipe Wells Village. It is very rough going and unmarked. At the head of this canyon, Lemoigne built a rock cabin and worked a silver claim that paid only meager returns. He died on one of his trips out and was buried near Salt Creek. Since then nothing has been done at the claim. It is ten miles from Hwy. 190 junction to the head of the canyon. Wash-outs are frequent and one-half to all day should be allowed for this trip.

The first several miles up Cottonwood and Marble canyons are across deep sandy stretches. Upper portions of the canyon may allow or deny further travel even to a small jeep depending upon seasonal washouts. Trips to this are should be made after consultation with a Park Ranger and if you are prepared for more than a one day trip. From Stovepipe Wells Village it is about 8.0 miles to the entrance to the narrows. From there on, no pretense of a road is made. Both canyons head high up on Hunter Mountain junctioning with the road from Ulida Flat and Goldbelt Springs, going west to Jackass Springs and Grapevine Canyon. Cottonwood Canyon carries an intermittent stream providing water for many cottonwood trees and shrubs. They furnish food and shelter for many types of desert animals and birds. Indians use this as one of their retreats from the hot valley in midsummer.

SALT CREEK

The running stream between the Sand Dunes and the salt basin west of Park Service Headquarters flows all year. Through the low, colorful Salt Creek Hills, it is bordered by unusual salt-tolerant grasses. In this creek are thousands of small pupfish *(Cyprinodon salinus)*. An attractive outdoor exhibit has been arranged by the Park Service with boardwalks extending for more than a quarter of a mile along and over the stream.

Elsewhere in the Monument, similar fish are found at Saratoga Springs and to the east outside of the Monument at Devil's Hole. These fish live in fresh water. Their presence in three somewhat different areas reinforce the premise that these southwest basins were filled with interconnecting lakes in prehistoric times.

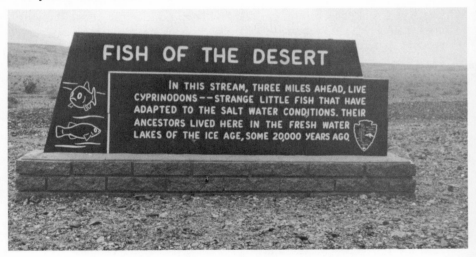

PIONEERS

It was for the wagon train of half-starved pioneers to record the beginning of the white man into this land. These emigrants pushed westward on a supposed shortcut to the newly discovered gold fields to enter Death Valley in the winter of 1849. They had deserted their guide and were lost in the wilderness, hungry and tired. As they came down Furnace Wash, the wide salt floor of the Valley with the towering Panamints beyond, was the last blow to their morale. The train separated into seven groups each seeking its own escape. One group, known as the Jayhawker Party, abandoned almost all its equipment, made its exit through a canyon later named the Jayhawkers, and crossed the Panamint Valley and Mojave Desert.

The Burned Wagon Historical Monument at Stovepipe Wells commemorates the passing of the '49ers. It was near here they had killed their oxen and broke up their wagons to use as fuel to jerky the meat for food. It was then divided up among them before they separated.

The Bennett-Arcane Party crossed the salt flats. They camped for 26 days at Tule Spring and nearly starved. William Lewis Manly and John Rogers were sent ahead in a desperate attempt to find a way to civilization and to bring aid if possible.

They finally returned with food and renewed hope and led their group to safety. Manly later wrote that the weary emigrants looked back across the valley—that tremendous barrier that had caused so much suffering for them and said, "Goodbye, Death Valley!" While some pioneers had lost their lives along the trail westward, only one emigrant died in Death Valley. What they had lost was their hope, which crumbled their spirits. By entering in winter, the most ideal time of the year to be in Death Valley, they had the maximum opportunity to survive in it. Later some of the forty-niners returned as guides or as prospectors to search for the Lost Gunsight silver lode or as John Goler did, to seek his canyon of gold.

CENTRAL DEATH VALLEY

Sand Dunes Jctn. - Badwater
Furnace Creek Ranch/Visitor Center
Dante's View - Greenwater Valley

BIG DUNE

← Beatty

LATHROP WELLS
2640

3812

Indian Pass

FUNERAL

TERS PEAK
5033
ES PEAK

3940

5969

Canyon

Echo

SCHWAUB PEAK
6448

MOUNTAINS

Amargosa

Scranton Well

River

Imvite
2250

Franklin Well

2255

e Point

2720

Hole in the Wall

6703 PYRAMID PEA.

49er PARTY ROUTE

4.5

2430

Water

?

2.4

1.5

American
Borate Mine

Ryan Mine
4423

Borax Mines

18

3000

4521

Kelleys Well

49ER ROUTE Old RR Grade

**DEATH VALLEY
JCTN.**

190

Lila C Mine

6.5

Shosh.

Long Pine

Natural
Bridge

R
A
N
G
E

GREENWATER

5.0

G
R
E
E
N
W
A
T
E
R

4525

17.0

6.0

DANTES
VIEW

02

COFFIN PEAK
5503

3.0

5/48

Greenwater Canyon

3468

FURNACE

3.5

VALLEY

Baker

71

Mines
GREENWATER

4.0

2.3

Coffin Canyon

CENTRAL AREA

FURNACE CREEK RANCH area, be sure to visit the . . . .

Museum, the Death Valley National Monument's Visitor's Center with panoramic displays and Naturalists' programs, see the old stages and wagons, and "Old Dinah" the specially designed traction steam engine that could not do the work of the mule team.

At the Ranch is a store, swimming pool, coffee shop, cabins, ice and service station. Texas Springs Campground has space for trailers as well as for tents. The Furnace Creek Inn provides luxury accommodations including gift shop, dining room and swimming pool.

HARMONY BORAX WORKS and MUSTARD CANYON. Boilers, old tanks and adobe walls are all that remain of the first borax operations in Death Valley. Out in the salt flats are old rows of borax once scooped up by Chinese laborers.

The Mustard Canyon loop allows a close view of the salt crusted mud hills which are deposits from the ancient Lake Manly that once covered the entire floor of Death Valley.

Furnace Creek Ranch - Badwater

This popular tour is enjoyed best if the visitor first goes all the way down to Badwater. There in the mid-morning hours the lights and shadows are at their greatest advantage for picture taking.

The long, steep climb up the fan to the Natural Bridge as well as the trip out to the Salt Pools should be taken in the cool of the morning.

Also, the one-way road through Artist's Drive must be taken by entry from the south. Both this drive and Golden Canyon are at their best intensity of color in the last afternoon when the sun begins to dip closer to the Panamint Range casting contrasting shadows and highlighting the golden glow.

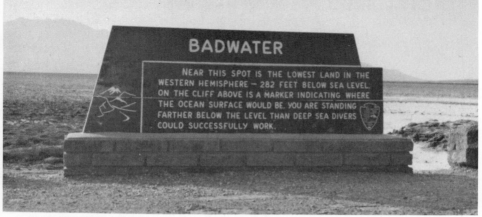

BADWATER. The extremes of old and new exist side by side. In the great cliffs reaching high to the east are found some of the oldest rocks in the world, while just south at the head of the spreading fan can be seen a parallel fault scarp formed during the past century. The Badwater pool, 280′ below sea level reflects Telescope Peak, 11,049′ above sea level. The source of this water is subterranean emitting from the cliffs.

In this barren, forbidding place lies the composite features of the Death Valley legend. Here, contrasts in the land are exaggerated in color and form. Glistening flatlands reach out from towering, lifeless cliffs. Across the desolation of waterless wastes and unbearable summer heat lies the late afternoon shadow of snowcapped Telescope Peak. Here is the place where the legend takes form and becomes a reality.

Above, although not visible from Badwater is Dante's View, 5,475′. The white sign high up on the cliffs shows the location of sea level. Above that can be seen the ice age lake waterline, 600 feet above the pool.

Further contrast is given between the barren, lifeless appearing salt flats to the west and the variety of living things that make this strange place their habitat. In the pool live tiny algae, leech-like larva of the horsefly, mollusks and other species of invertibrate life. In the briny soil bordering the pool is found salt grass and the leafless pickleweed. Nearby, above the road is found desert holly saltbush, spurge and honeysweet plants.

NATURAL BRIDGE. A great arch resulting from erosional forces cutting through the old alluvial fan deposits that had been uplifted to form a dam across the canyon. Cloudburst run-offs undermined the dam leaving the natural bridge composed of concreted materials. (The bridge is just around the turn about 300 yards up the canyon from the end of the road.)

SALT POOLS. Here are salt crystals forming out of the clear brine in open pools. These pools were formed when the water level beneath the surface was high, dissolving the salt making vertical channels some hundreds of feet deep. On the surface of the salt can be seen small mound holes, 2" to 3" in diameter, which are breathers caused by respiration of the water as it surges back and forth during times of local earth movement.

ARTIST'S DRIVE. One of the most beautiful trips in Death Valley. It provides a great panorama of brilliantly colored hills and knolls, a closeup of the towering fault scarp forming the wall to the east of the basin and Artist's Palette—a maze of intensely colored mounds that gives the Point its name.

It is a region of overlapping and tumbled lakebed sediments and volcanics. There are more than a dozen shades of pastel colors; the reds and the yellows result from iron rust, the black from manganese dioxide and the green from the chlorides remaining from the disintegration of mica.

GOLDEN CANYON. Formed by faulting and carved by erosion, its walls are striking in their vivid, golden colors. This unusually high coloration is due to the oxidation of iron in the rocks and soil. The surface of these deposits is clay which, being nearly impervious to water, allows much of the rainfall to run off immediately. Eroding or wearing away of the clay by small rivulets has developed deep gullies. The more resistant layers of gravel and lava have worn away less rapidly and stand out prominently as ridges and layers of contrasting color. From the end of the road, trails lead to the base of Cathedral Wall and Manly Beacon.

Rocky Rockwell

The West Side Road is rough and dusty and the water from the wells and springs are not too pleasant for drinking. This route crosses the Valley floor through Devils Golf Course, past the old campsites of the Forty-Niner Party, the graves of Jim Dayton and Shorty Harris and the site of the old Eagle Borax Works.

DEVILS GOLF COURSE. As the waters from Lake Manly evaporated, its salts became more concentrated. They cracked into irregular blocks during the drying process, which were tilted and raised by the force of the recrystallization of the salt. Wind-driven rains eroded these into sharp ridges, peaks, and pinnacles. Although only a few feet high, the roughness is extreme, presenting a barrier to man and beast.

At Saratoga Springs the quiet loneliness of this vast desert basin brings close the feeling that must have haunted the lost pioneers from the specter of death that had been their constant companion.

In the warm fresh water springs are many tiny fish—cousins to those found far to the north in the briny Salt Creek near the Sand Dunes and Stovepipe Wells area.

THROUGH THIS NATURAL GATEWAY THE DEATH VALLEY
FORTY-NINERS, MORE THAN ONE HUNDRED EMIGRANTS
FROM THE MIDDLE WEST, SEEKING A SHORT CUT TO
GOLD FIELDS OF CENTRAL CALIFORNIA, ENTERED
DEATH VALLEY, DECEMBER, 1849. ALL SUFFERED
FROM THIRST AND STARVATION. TWO CONTINGENTS
PASSED SOUTHWARD HERE, THE OTHERS PROCEEDED
NORTHWARD SEEKING TO ESCAPE FROM REGION

At the Junction of Highway 190 and the road to Badwater stands a stone monument to the '49ers. They entered Death Valley through this pass on Christmas Day in 1849. They had come down Furnace Creek Wash from Death Valley Junction.

The last campsite of the pioneers before attempting to cross the Valley floor was at TRAVERTINE SPRINGS. The warm stream now flows down to provide water for the swimming pool at the Inn and to irrigate the date palm grove at the Ranch. The springs are "original water"—a condensation from underground volcanic steam which forms flowing springs that are active the year around.

ZABRISKIE POINT. A parking circle overlooks a panorama of "badlands"—old lake bed sediments, volcanic flows and alluvial fan materials—which when combined, form a land as strange as the surface of the moon. In fact, this area has been the setting for many science fiction motion pictures.

Manly Beacon was named after William Lewis Manly, the member of the '49ers party who used this vantage point to scout the lay of the land to the west. Both he and John Rogers did find the way to lead the pioneers out.

Early morning and late afternoon are the best time for photography since contrasting shadows on the barren hills are at their best. Usually, the sunsets over the Panamint Range from Zabriskie Point are most spectacular and memorable.

TWENTY-MULE TEAM CANYON. Through this canyon the 20-mule team outfits hauled colemanite borax in the '80's. The old boarding house, now used as the Museum at Furnace Creek Ranch, was located on a small flat about two miles from the road.

The eroded low hills are soft and crumbly. The yellow and white clay material makes an interesting color contrast when seen against the vari-colored rocks of the Black Mountains beyond.

After leaving Hwy. 190, the road to Dante's View and Greenwater Valley is flanked on both sides by interesting historical activities typical of the borax mining days. To the west, in the Black Mountains, are old mine workings and prospecting tunnels. To the east, in the Funeral Mountains, are the buildings and old railroad grades of the RYAN MINE operated by the Pacific Coast Borax Company between 1914 to 1928.

In these mountains are the original source of borate in Death Valley. The entire mountain of lakebed sediments was formed by uplifting earth movements. Lava was deposited over the folded playa, making the area a colorful mixture of reds, yellows, browns and greens.

DANTE'S VIEW is one of the most exhilerating sights anywhere. A wide range of naked canyons, alluvial fans and the vast salt flats can be seen. The morning or evening is the best time to fully appreciate it. This viewpoint is about a mile high, just as it is a mile below the summit of Telescope Peak (11,045'). The green spots below to the southwest are Mesquite and Bennett's Wells, while over to your right the green patch is Furnace Creek Ranch.

Off to the right is the Whitney View Trail leading to the spot where the highest and the lowest points of this section of the United States can be seen. (Mt. Whitney—14,495' above sea level; Badwater—280' below sea level.)

For a side trip, visit Greenwater and Furnace. These are two ghost towns of copper mining days—once so alive with hopes and dreams, now so empty in the desert sun. The roads are passable, although dirt. This route is seldom patrolled.

SOUTHEAST AREA

Southern Death Valley
Black Mountains
Badwater - Saratoga Springs
Baker/Las Vegas Roads via Shoshone

SOUTHEAST ENTRY INTO DEATH VALLEY NATIONAL MONUMENT

Baker, 50 miles east of Barstow on Hwy. I-15, provides the shortest route to those wishing to explore the lower Death Valley Basin. At Baker is a shaded park with tables. It is about 100 miles into Death Valley through the upper Mojave and lower Amargosa deserts. In early spring the wildflower show is outstanding.

From the Ibex Pass route (Hwy. 127 north from Baker) are entries to numerous backcountry jeep trips on unimproved, dirt, seldom patrolled roads. There are many old mine sites and remote weekend camping spots in the Ibex Hills. Another good trip would be to turn off just below Ripple Dunes going into lower Death Valley to the Saratoga Springs area. The Greenwater Valley road is unpaved, dusty, and not patrolled below its junction with Dante's View Road. Just north of Ashford Mill junction is a good jeep road into the Butte Valley and Anvil Spring via Warm Springs Canyon.

GREENWATER—A True Ghost Town.

Even when it was operating at its best, all the "Greatest Copper Camp on Earth" had was dreams and the ghost of what might have been, but never became. It was going to be the copper center of the world, only "there wasn't enough good copper to make a tea kettle". The camp consisted of boarding houses, general stores, bank, hardware and drug store, two newspapers, telephone, and telegraph lines. The development money poured in from investors before the proving of any ore—it was such a sure thing! There was no water. What they did get they had to haul from Furnace Creek some 25 miles away. Railroads planned spur lines to it but they were never built. Mines were financed that never existed.

The population was made up mostly of Nevada boomers who lived in tents with dirt floors. The weather was impossible. So hot in the summer even the lizards were sunburned; so cold in winter men had to sleep in their clothes and spent all their waking hours scrounging for sagebrush to cook their meals and keep from freezing. Their companions came from the nearby rocks at night—sidewinders, scorpions, centipedes and lizards. Most of the year the wind blew twenty-four hours a day. Hot dust and sandstorms whipped their tents. It blew one way all day unceasingly then, after a short, quiet spell when it turned around someplace out on the Amargosa flats, then blew all night the other way.

Some twenty years ago I visited the old Greenwater camp. There were tumbled rock walls, rusted tin cans, and great mounds of shattered beer and whiskey bottles. They may have been short on water but they certainly weren't short on drink! Over the desolate scene could be found great holes in the ground where, for a short time, they dug furiously like hungry badgers, then moved on to a new place. It was sublime that spring day. So quiet one could hear the movement of a lizard nearby crossing the soft sand. Birds sang in the sage. For miles intermittent patches of flowers colored the harsh desert waste of the Amargosa. We looked at the pitiful remains of empty holes and unfulfilled dreams and realized man's deeds and destruction last longer than man himself.

Looking over the few scattered remnants of mining activity, it is hard to realize that a city of 1,000 people was here. Stores, hotels, saloons, newspaper office, boarding houses and, yes, even a drug store once made up the city.

THE BORAX STORY

In the shimmering heat of the desert sun the floor of Death Valley climaxed the despair of the lost '49ers and harassed the gold-searching burro-prospectors. With visions of riches from the nearby hills they crossed and recrossed the Valley's glistening flats unaware of the fortune in the "white gold" spread around them. Few had heard of Marco Polo and the precious white crystals of borax he had so carefully brought back from Mongolia so many centuries before.

Used by Venetian goldsmiths as a flux in the welding of precious stones on the shields and crowns of noblemen and kings, it was in the packs of overland camel caravans from the Far East. Its value had been known by the ancient Babylonians and Persians some two thousand years ago. For over sixteen centuries China utilized borax in their glazes for the exquisite, delicate porcelain.

The Death Valley Borax Story began in 1880 when Aaron Winters and his wife Rosie, learned from a passing prospector that there were riches in the white stuff called borax. It had been found elsewhere in California before the Civil War and later in Nevada. Searles Lake had been processing salines since 1878. However, it was Winter's discovery in Death Valley that opened up the new day in borax mining in the west. True to the habit of most prospectors, the Winters sold out for $20,000 and bought a big ranch at Pahrump. The buyer, William Coleman, soon developed the first sizeable mining operations in Death Valley. It became known as the Harmony Borax Works and, to support its activities, he expanded the Greenfield Ranch— now called Furnace Creek Ranch. Both the borax works and the ranch enjoyed good fortune by having an enormous supply of running water from springs up Furnace Creek Wash.

The "cottonball" was gathered by Chinese laborers with simple tools such as racks, scoopers, and shovels. It was then loaded into two-wheel carts and hauled to the reduction vats at Harmony. During the summer months ground temperatures reached as high as 170°. Another borax operation began at Eagle Borax Springs at the southwest side of the Valley but it was short lived due to poor management. When deposits were discovered at Amargosa, due to its higher elevation, Coleman could operate there in the summer and at Harmony in the winter.

The crudely refined borax was hauled to railroad sidings farther south at Daggett and Mojave. Small mule teams soon expanded into extensive operations known as the 20-Mule Team outfits. Huge high-wheeled wagons, drawn by the teams were built to do the special job of transporting the borates to the railroad terminals. Each wagon was 16' long, 4' wide, and 6' deep, and capable of carrying ten tons of borax. The back wheels were 7' in diameter the forwards ones 5'. The heavy iron tires were 8" wide and an inch thick. Empty wagons weighed 7800 pounds each and cost $900. Special teams hauled feed to ten overnight camp stations along the 165-mile route. The large teams covered between 15-17 miles each day, depending on the weather. It took about 20 days to make a round trip.

An effort was made to reduce costs and problems of using the mules by constructing a huge steam tractor to pull the wagons. But it was no match for the mule-team with the great heat and low humidity. Today, Old Dinah can be seen at the entrance to the Furnace Creek Ranch. More deposits of higher grade ore were discovered to the east up Furnace Creek Wash. The Lila C. Mine was only one hundred miles from Ivanpah—the Santa Fe Railroad junction. Coleman built a wagon road to it and reactivated Old Dinah but it failed fourteen miles from the end of the road on the first trip so the 20-mule teams had to take over.

In the map the heavy solid line shows the main borax route between Harmony Borax Works and Mojave. The broken line denotes the Amargosa-Daggett route and the route sometimes followed between Harmony and Daggett. Square dots mark the routes of the Searles Lake-Mojave trains. The light dotted line shows probably the oldest route, followed by Ed Stiles between Eagle Borax Works and Daggett. The much shorter Borate-Daggett run is indicated by the light solid line.

Competition and the need for more efficient transportation led to the building of the Tonopah and Tidewater railroad out of Las Vegas in 1905 to service the Lila C. and the Tonopah and Goldfield mines. A branch line, the Death Valley Railroad connected the Ryan Mine operations with Death Valley Junction between 1914 and 1928. A baby-gauge railroad ran deep into the mountains and along the steep hillside for three and a half miles. The new Ryan became the center of borax mining in the United States producing annually some $2-$3 million. Operations were suspended in 1928 when the company began production at the new location at Boron.

This major change in the borax industry took place when the new source was discovered thirty miles east of Mojave—at Boron—almost at the very spot that had been the end of the line of the 20-mule outfit from Death Valley. A homesteader, trying to find a good supply of fresh water for his ranch struck colemanite instead. Acquired by the borax company, it was at first operated on the conventional method of room-and-pillar underground development. Since 1957 its activity has enlarged to gigantic proportions when it changed to the open-pit mining.

In 1971 Tenneco, Inc. a Houston-based conglomerate with unlimited capital, began extensive strip mining for borate ore in Death Valley by the open-pit method. It began by making a hole more than a half mile long. Questions then arose as to its permanent damage to the esthetic environment of the region. Legislation that established the Valley and its environs as a National Monument had not anticipated the machinery or effect of open-pit operations from existing claims that were never voided. The mine is now operated under the name of American Borate Company with indications that it will be mined underground rather than open-pit. The burro-prospector never envisioned the character of today's earth moving equipment. Hopefully, a working arrangement can be developed that will settle the problem before it is too late to save this unique region from complete disaster.

Old 20-Mule Team Road Across Death Valley

DAYLIGHT PASS-BEATTY ROAD

In early spring the broad alluvial fan between the Valley and Hell's Gate junction is usually carpeted with dwarf flowers. The area between the Grapevine and Funeral Mountains presents one of the most easily reached and finest panoramic views of the Death Valley sink.

Death Valley Buttes, a landmark to travelers in early days, was also a suggested location of the famous Lost Breyfogle Lode that has never been found. East of Hell's Gate the road is steeper and then winds around many low hills through Boundary Canyon to Daylight Pass (4317'). Morning and evening shadows enhance the gray and red bands on Corkscrew Peak.

Both the Keane Wonder and Chloride Cliffs mines in the Funeral Mountains were active around 1900 to 1916. There had been some mining in the early years before the 1870's at Chloride City, but the first commercial mining operations in Death Valley weren't until the 1900's. Nestled in the shallow basin surrounded by the peaks of the Funerals was Chloride City. Water for the mines as well as for the city was piped from the Keane Springs just three miles north. Because the water was so precious and the citizens so unsavory, the pipeline was constantly patrolled.

CHLORIDE CLIFFS is reached by a trail south of the old city site. The trip to the top is well worth the effort since the view is really spectacular— the Panamints, the Sierra Nevada, Telescope and Death Valley.

South of the cliffs a jeep road leads to the Gold Dollar Mine site. The first road to Death Valley was from Mojave and Barstow to Chloride City but sands and time have wiped away most of the traces.

KEANE WONDER. Two years before Shorty Harris discovered Bullfrog, the Keane Wonder Mine was operating. By 1907 a 20-stamp mill was necessary to crush the rich ore. The mine is about a mile up from the mill. The tramway and mill site can be explored but with caution. Faulty buttressed tunnels, unsupported ceilings and old mining shafts—unmarked deep holes, are scattered among the desert landscape. The Keane Wonder Mine's total output was estimated at about $1 million.

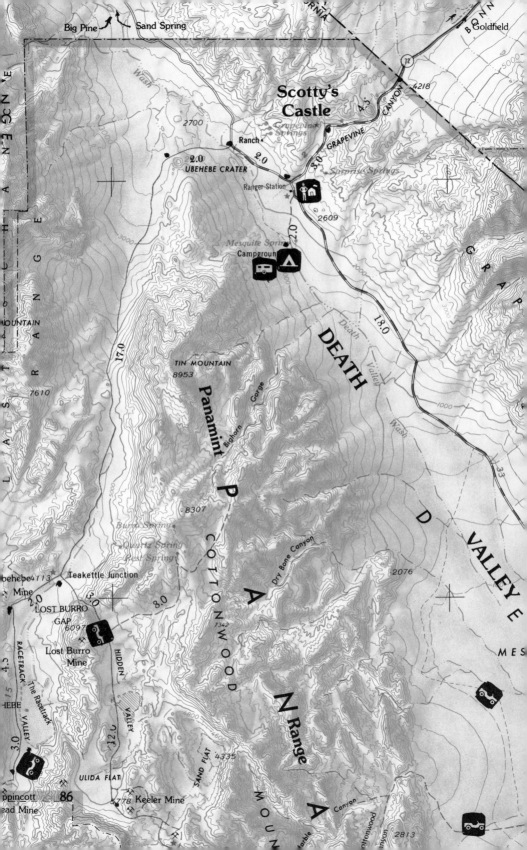

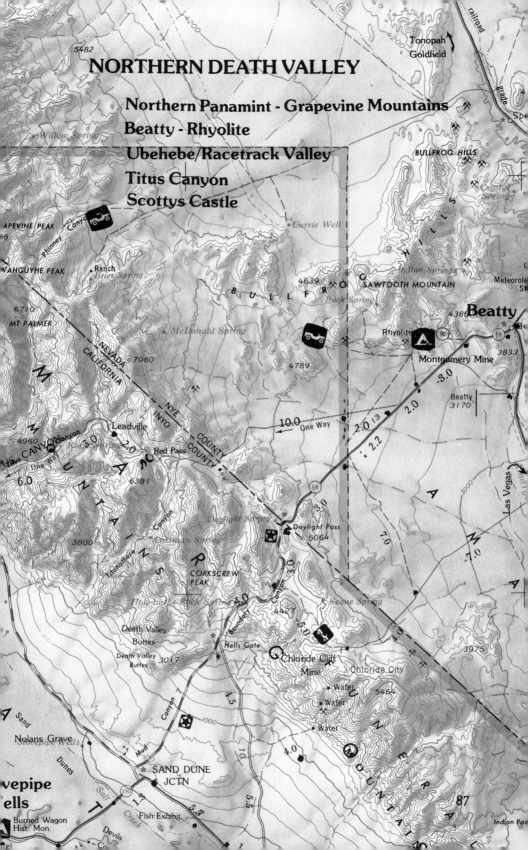

RHYOLITE - BULLFROG

Shorty Harris was a prospector's idea of what a real prospector should be—a dreamer with an uncanny knack of actually finding rich ore. He never became common enough to be a miner. He shared his discoveries with others as easily as if it were only a drink of water at a desert spring. He always had a partner whether in a saloon or looking for gold. And so it was in 1904 when he, with a partner he picked up at the Keane Wonder mine, set out across the valley from Daylight Springs to explore the mountains that were to become the Bullfrog Hills. It was there he found the big one. The one he had been looking for all those years.

The arrival of Harris and Cross in Goldfield with samples of almost pure gold ignited a rush like a Hollywood movie. They came on foot pushing wheelbarrows loaded with supplies and tools, on burros, and a few lucky ones in wagons. The gold was found in bright green rock—hence the name Bullfrog. The exodus from Goldfield soon had the new strike "staked" with claims for miles around and the boom was on.

Whatever the record shows about the dreams, stock promotion deals, or its isolation in the desert, Rhyolite was never meant to be a "shanty town". A visit to this remote, empty, desert valley shows plenty of proof of the determination of the builders who planned this town that it would last. From the beginning it was laid out to become the biggest city in western Nevada. Streets were surveyed and arranged in orderly fashion. Many claims were located, railroads were built, stores and office buildings were made of stone and concrete to serve notice that this place was here to stay. It was not to be. Poetically speaking, the bridegroom had made all the plans for a great honeymoon, but the bride never showed up at the church. Except for a couple of mines the rest was only hopeful ventures.

It was a period when people wanted to believe. There had been so many times they had almost made it. They had been close at Nevada City, Virginia City, Tonopah, and Goldfield. The first claims promised so much. The very color of the hills gave assurance of a great strike. It became a race "to get in on the ground floor before all the others got there." So, a city was built upon the drifting sands of hope.

Nearby other camps and towns such as Bullfrog, Amargosa and Bonanza were made up of loose stone walls and hillside dug-outs. Competition between the settlements of Bullfrog and Rhyolite became stiff. With free lots to the first comers and the coming of the Las Vegas & Tonopah Railroad to Rhyolite, Bullfrog faded fast.

The Bullfrog mine and the Montgomery-Shoshone were the best in the area. The Bullfrog produced the excitement and the Montgomery more than $2 million. It also produced some of the trickiest stock swindle deals that has been devised in those imaginative times. Shorty sold his half of the claim to the first good buyer. Cross hung on to his and got enough to buy a ranch down near San Diego where he retired.

The leasing system was not used at the Rhyolite-Bullfrog mines. With the recent rich strikes at Tonopah and Goldfield, excitement was at a new high. Everyone wanted to put all they had into the new venture. Stock market operators at San Francisco and in the east competed to get in on the action before it was too late. Montgomery sold out to Charles S. Schwab, president of the U.S. Steel Corporation for some $2 million then he re-invested half of it back into the operations. The mine played out in five years having produced some $2 million—almost enough to pay its debts in building the big mill.

It was a time of great speculators. Millions of shares of stock issued at a par value of $1.00 was doubled within a few weeks and not worth the cost of the paper it was printed on within a few months. The speculators who invested millions in stocks were left with only dreams of what might have been. "All that glitters isn't gold!" was never more truly said than here. The glowing report of mine operators trying to sell out matched the multi-colored hills surrounding the valley. When week after week went by and assay reports showed less and less, the great exodus began.

These Nevada mines fell because they were not as rich as supposed, and their stock was oversold. The fire in San Francisco and the Wall Street depression made further investments unprofitable and almost overnight the entire enterprise collapsed. Everyone was in such a rush to get out many of the people walked away with what they could carry leaving all the rest of their household and property behind.

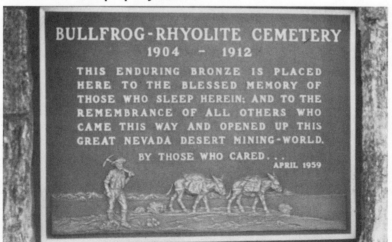

Today's Rhyolite remains one of our most visible ghost towns. A few residents operate tourist shops and help in saving the valley from plundering. Samples of ores and relics of the past are on exhibit at both Bullfrog and the Bottle House. Most noticeable are the stark walls of the tall bank building standing like strange monuments in the broad sage-covered valley. The large stone depot is one of the best preserved in the west. Today it is a bar. The old cemetery located about a mile south of Bullfrog tells its own story. Those who sought riches of the mines found peace in the solitude of this quiet land. Some of the remaining headboards are too weathered to be read. The fences once placed to keep off the wandering coyote now must withstand the souvenir hunter.

Bottlehouse at Rhyolite

Old Railroad Depot at Rhyolite

Red Pass (Bloody Gap) Titus Canyon Country

The TITUS CANYON road twists down a graveled bottom wash between towering walls. These show the faulting and the tilting of the earth, the grinding and the polishing from cloudburst torrents. Some high-water marks and driftwood embedded in the canyon walls tell the story of the ferocity of nature on the loose. This is no place to be during a thunderstorm.

When the Leadfield ore was first discovered this was the only way into and out of the area. Supplies for the mines and the town had to be brought in through Death Valley and patiently hauled up this difficult route, with a rise of 5500' in only eleven miles.

The road from Rhyolite to Leadfield crosses a wide, open desert divide, dips down between colored hills and climbs over Bloody Gap or Red Pass. Bones of huge prehistoric mammals have been found in the Titanothere Canyon just south of here in the Grapevine Mountains. This is a one-way road going west. There are some sharp, steep pitches, and in places very narrow. It is no road for large RV units and trailers!

Miner's Dugout at Leadville

NPS Photo

LEADFIELD was doomed from the start. It was a stock promotion deal to "take" the boys on Wall Street which they proceeded to do to the tune of several million dollars. In this land and times where all things were possible, the poor did become rich and the rich became poor! Fantasies of the treasure seeker following the "yellow brick road" became real and unreal events became legends. Steamboats in the desert? Of course! They appeared on posters of the Stock Exchange in Chicago and New York enticing speculators to invest huge fortunes in the stocks of Leadfield. The ships were shown loaded with bullion drifting down Titus Canyon, to the Amargosa River, across Mojave to the seaport of Los Angeles. Ah me, what a day!

Only a few foundations and scattered debris—boards, rusted metal and unproductive tunnels are left. Even the shack pictured has been long gone.

KLARE SPRINGS is marked by a patch of tules. This was the main water supply of Leadfield. On the rock walls can be found Indian writings of those who camped here long ago.

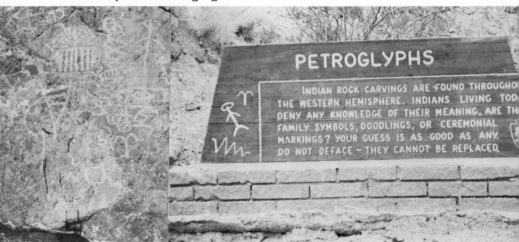

SCOTTYS CASTLE

This provincial Spanish castle is a monument to the incredulous nature of Death Valley and to the people of those times. Amid nature's vast outdoor museum stands a fabulous man-made museum of art—in paintings, architecture, ceramics, woodcraft, and furnishings—treasures from all over the world. The National Park Service has guided tours for a nominal fee which is used for the upkeep of the castle. There are gift shops, a gas station and a large parking area among the tamarack trees for a shady rest.

That Death Valley Scotty was ever a real prospector is open to many doubts. That he had a secret gold mine in Death Valley and built a fabulous castle in Grapevine Canyon with its returns, there can be no doubt—it just didn't happen that way. That he was a genial, windy promoter who liked to talk and entertain people with grandiose yarns, there is no question there. He was a champion at that. His years with Buffalo Bill's Wild West Show taught him much that sharpened his talents to show off.

So typical of Scotty and the times in which he lived was the stunt he pulled Sunday afternoon, July 9, 1905 when he walked into a railroad station in Los Angeles and plunked down a bag of money at the ticket window with the request that he wanted to rent a train—the whole train, not just a seat, and he wanted to set a record between there and Chicago. Scotty's "gold mine" had put up the cash, the Santa Fe Railroad people grasped at the chance of such free publicity.

It took 19 engines, 19 engineers, 10 conductors, 18 firemen, a company of dispatchers and switchmen to pull it off. The unit included a baggage car, a dining car and a pullman. They left Los Angeles at 1:00 PM July 9, and arrived in Chicago at 11:54 AM, July 11, 1905—a distance of 2265 miles in 44 hours and 54 minutes! The route included Albuquerque, Dodge City and Kansas City. People of every city and "whistle-stop" hamlet turned out to cheer him on as he whizzed through. On the way he wired President Teddy Roosevelt, "An American cowboy is coming East on a special train faster than any cowpuncher ever rode before...."

No, there was nothing shy or lacking about Scotty except modesty and a real honest-to-goodness gold mine in Death Valley! (The money for the venture had been put up by a Los Angeles real estate speculator to publicize mining promotion opportunities in the Mojave Desert. Scotty's Castle was actually built by Albert Johnson, a retired Chicago insurance company executive who had been talked into coming west for his health by Scotty.)

93

UBEHEBE CRATER (Indian meaning: Big Basket in the Rock). It is an inverted cone, a half-mile in width at the top, 800 feet deep and 450 feet wide at the base. It literally "blew its top" some one thousand years ago. Because of its explosive action the horizontal layers of rock in the crater walls are clearly seen. Debris is scattered in volcanic ash and stone for a radius of three miles from the crater. Just south of Ubehebe are smaller, younger craters—only several hundred years old.

A trail leads to the bottom of Ubehebe. The red and orange layers framed by the pale gray and ocher walls piled layer upon layer are most spectacular. The slopes surrounding the craters are covered with black cinders. Here the silver-gray desert holly grows in scattered profusion giving a most beautiful contrast of dark and light, barrenness and life.

RACETRACK VALLEY

This is an unusual trip that includes the area lying between the Cottonwood Mountains and the Last Chance Range. It is reached by an undeveloped dirt road that is rough in places. However, with care and allowing all day for the trip rewards are well worth it. Between Ubehebe and Teakettle Junction are found numerous cacti and plants typical of high desert valleys where late spring produces wildflower displays seldom seen in the lower valleys. Take your time through here, and plenty of film. It is a desert garden at its best.

The moving rocks of Racetrack Valley have long been the subject of speculation by visitors and scientists. Numerous rocks ranging in size of a basketball to some weighing more than five hundred pounds have left smooth trails in different directions across the old lakebed. Early stories crediting this movement to hidden magnetic forces or "pull" were later disproved. In recent years studies have been made that claim the most likely cause of their movement is the result of strong wind action. The old playa becomes exceedingly slick during a light rainstorm. If followed by a sustained period of hurricane force winds, the rocks could be pushed along leaving the trails behind them.

There are numerous abandoned mines in the southern end of Racetrack Valley, Hidden Valley, and Goldbelt Spring. Remember, trips into the Cottonwood Mountains are hazardous and unpatrolled, and that you are a long way from any help.

Sand Dunes, Eureka Valley

Rocky Rockwell

EUREKA VALLEY

Lying between Cowhorn Valley and Last Chance Range this area is a last frontier of isolated, desert wilderness. In the southern end of the Valley, some fourteen miles south of the Cowhorn-Sand Springs road, are the largest sand dunes in California and the highest in the Basin Range country. They are three and a half miles long, one mile wide, and over six hundred and eighty feet high. A special, rare, and endemic grass found nowhere else in the world has successfully developed in the dunes (shown on the front inside cover). There is a wide variety of other desert plants and wildlife in this beautiful dune area. Travel is limited to the established roadway.

SALINE VALLEY

This is a primitive desert valley and mountain association where the influence impact of modern man is not in evidence. It is significant geologically, outstanding scenically and almost unique as a desert valley in its original state. Until recently only prospectors ever visited Saline Valley. It was more of a menace to people than people were to the valley. It is the last unspoiled desert area. BLM has restricted recreational use by rescuing it in time with limiting travel to designated roads and trails only.

The floor of the valley was mined for borax years ago but these deposits were exhausted before the turn of the century. A tramway was built over the Inyo escarpment in 1912 to get salt which was so pure it was sold without refining. The enterprise fell into bad times. Part of the tramway is still in existence to show evidence of this monumental endeavor. There are eight active mining claims on the flanks of the mountain rimming Saline Valley.

95

Joshua Trees in the Darwin Hills

DESERT LIFE

That Death Valley has not always had such an arid climate is generally recognized as we look over the shoreline markings of ancient lakes in the salt flats. We can easily assume that plant life was also somewhat different. The extent of this has been emphasized as fossil remains of animals are found in several places in the Monument. In Titus Canyon near Leadfield have been found fossils of the titantherium, a small horse, dogs, tapers, brontotheres, and small rodents. In the great wash near Emigrant Station are found fossil fish and gastropods (snails). North of Ubehebe Crater part of the tusk of a mastodon was found in the clay beds of ancient Lake Rogers. In Copper Canyon are scores of fossil footprints of birds, camels, small horses and mastodon tracks. One area includes so many animal footprints it is often referred to as "the barnyard". Reeds, grasses and other vegetation have also been found. Out near the Amargosa River fossilized palm leaves and stems have been discovered.

The variety, number, and size of those animals indicate the presence of a climate where a large variety and quantity of plants once flourished. One of the most interesting remains of this former tropical environment can be observed at Salt Creek where thousands of tiny pupfish live. They are the only living creatures whose ancestral lineage can be traced back to the fish that inhabited Lake Manly during the Ice Age. They have survived through continued adaptation to environmental changes while those unable to adapt have faded and left only fossilized footprints in the barren canyons. Today's desert plant and animal life is an intriguing story of specialized methods of survival.

There are some 600 species of plants within the boundaries of Death Valley, with only the salt flats barren. Because of the adverse growing conditions, desert areas have a number of unusual and rare species. These plants have adapted strange mechanisms which keep them alive in the burning heat and dryness of summer. What moisture they do get is conserved by decreasing the evaporation surfaces through the elimination of leaves, by varnished or fuzz-covered leaf surfaces to detract sun rays, or by the shedding of their leaves in summer. Some plants combine two or more of these adaptations, and almost all the larger plants have roots that either penetrate deeply or spread far from the plant base.

When winter rains have been sufficient and the temperatures are just right spring flowers transform the alluvial fans, washes, and canyons from dull gray and somber brown into a spectrum of color. Sunflowers, white and yellow primroses present colorful patterns. Poppy fields and cacti delight the eye. Sturdy blossoms stand for days, but some fragile plants burst their buds in a blaze of splendor and are gone with the setting sun. Scattered seeds lie in the dust-dry soil to await the favoring rains of some following year.

The most common plants in the low country are desert holly, saltbush, and cresote bush. These drought resistant shrubs are widely scattered on the gravelly fans so that they do not use too much of the scanty water supply. The Death Valley sage, known only in this region, grows in the shady, dry canyons. Cacti which includes beavertail, pricklypear, cottontop, and cholla, have forsaken leaves altogether and broadened their stems to perform the same functions. Plants drop their leaves in the summer and grow during the winter. Some plants like the trumpet vine retains its water supply and siphons moisture as needed.

Twenty-six species of mammals live in Death Valley. Many are so adapted that they obtain all the moisture they need from their food. Antelope ground squirrels, wood rats, and rabbits inhabit the mesquite thickets and the fans. In the extreme heat of summer they retreat into the sand or rocky shelters out of the direct sunlight and wait out the long, hot summer in a stage of semi-hibernation. Lizards hibernate in winter and they range in size from the harmless chuckawalla to the tiny, banded gecko. Snakes are comparatively rare as the valley floor is too hot for them during the summer. Many of the birds seen are migrants—winter visitors—which include a number of water birds. Some fourteen species make the valley floor their permanent home, others live in the higher canyons. Most frequently seen is the large black American raven.

Saratoga Spring

PRINCIPAL PLANT ENVIRONMENTS

The types and profusion of plant life in the desert are affected by elevation, exposure, moisture, and kinds of soil. Between the crest of the Panamints at Telescope Peak (11,049') and Badwater (-282') unusual changes exist reflecting all these conditions.

 Bristlecone pine and Limber pine

 Pinyon-Juniper

 Upper Sonoran shrub zone

 Lower Sonoran zone xerophytes; especially creosote bush, with desert-holly at foot of the fans; burroweed at top of the highest ones.

 Phreatophytes, less salt tolerant than pickleweed; especially mesquite

 Pickleweed

 Bare ground on the saltpan

Spring

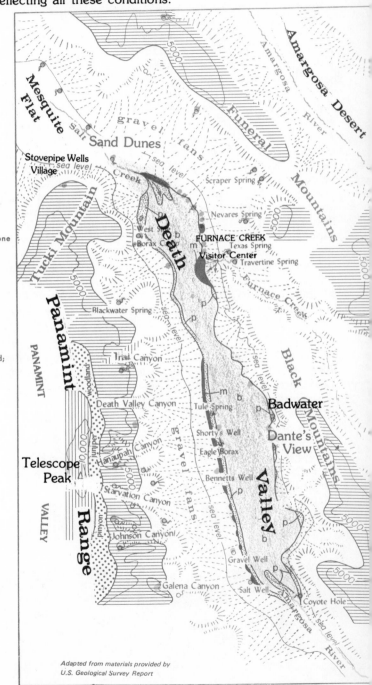

Adapted from materials provided by
U.S. Geological Survey Report

DESERT TRUMPET is a member of the Buckwheat family. From the basal cluster of leaves the main stem swells to contain a sticky liquid which provides nourishment to the plant during the dry season. Above the swelling, branches of tall, hollow stems bear tiny flowers.

DESERT HOLLY (Saltbush) is found in large numbers on washes and fans. It is quite tolerant of alkali and high salt-content soil. Its tough, glistening surface of leathery leaves reflects the brilliant desert sunlight and its sharp thorns discourage foraging animals. The resemblance to conventional holly gave it its name and also nearly caused its destruction. Before the Monument was established thousands of late fall visitors stripped the holly by the carloads to use as Christmas decor.

BEAVERTAIL PRICKLYPEAR is found in large numbers in the higher washes leading to Butte Valley and Racetrack Valley. Its flat, jointed stems dotted with tiny, stinging spines, perform the function of leaves. The beautiful magenta flowers develop along the edges of the stems.

COTTONTOP CACTUS grows in large colonies on alluvial fans. Very pulpy interior, exterior covered with long, thick spines. Small yellow flowers on heads are encased in white woolly fuzz—hence name.

MOJAVE DESERT-STAR belongs to the Sunflower family. Referred to as a "belly plant", it grows very close to the ground with short stems supporting a few dark green fuzzy leaves. The entire plant is 3"-4" across and presents a nosegay of a dozen or more tiny white flowers with yellow centers, similar to the daisy.

DESERT DANDELION with its butter yellow ce~~n~~ters in a pale yellow setting attract pollinating i~~n~~sects and the eager photographer. It has narro~~w~~ dark green leaves at crown level with flowers su~~p~~ported on tall stems. It grows best in sandy place~~s~~

MOJAVE ASTER gives a great display of lar~~ge~~ lavender colored flowers with yellow centers. The~~se~~ blossoms produce an amplitude of seeds to insu~~re~~ survival of the species. Foliage of a gray-green to~~ne~~ are spiny-toothed. A hardy shrub found in no~~n~~ alkaline soil in the southwestern desert slopes a~~nd~~ fans.

DESERT SENNA presents only a hard, barren st~~em~~ most of the year with no leaves or flowers. During ~~a~~ brief blooming season the stems put forth a ~~few~~ small leaves and a profusion of yellow blossom~~s~~

CHUCKAWALLA: One of the largest of our western lizards (it grows up to 15"-20"). Always found in rocky areas and is strictly vegetarian. A harmless, obtusive creature that escapes predators by taking refuge in tight places between rocks then inflating his body so he can't be dislodged. Attempts to drag him out by the tail are futile—his jointed tail separates from his body and in time a new one grows to replace it. Used by Indians and early prospectors as a staple food.

HORNED LIZARD (Horned Toad): Appears as a prehistoric monster but it is a harmless member of the lizard family. He is covered with rough, scaly skin and sharp horns to discourage being swallowed by a snake. Chief food is insects, ants, and flies. He was a great pet of the prospectors who encouraged them into the rocky shelters to help clear away spiders and ants.

SCORPION: An amber colored, crablike looking creature. Feeds on insects and bugs. Its elongated, jointed body contains a gland of venom. Capturing its victim with its claws, it injects the stinger before eating. Relatively harmless to humans, the sting is no more serious than from a bee or wasp. They seek dark places by day under rocks or in small burrows and forages at night.

DESERT TORTOISE: A most harmless vegetarian secures its moisture needs from the plants it eats. Extra water produced is carried in two small sacs on the back under its shell. They live to an unusual age of thirty years or more.

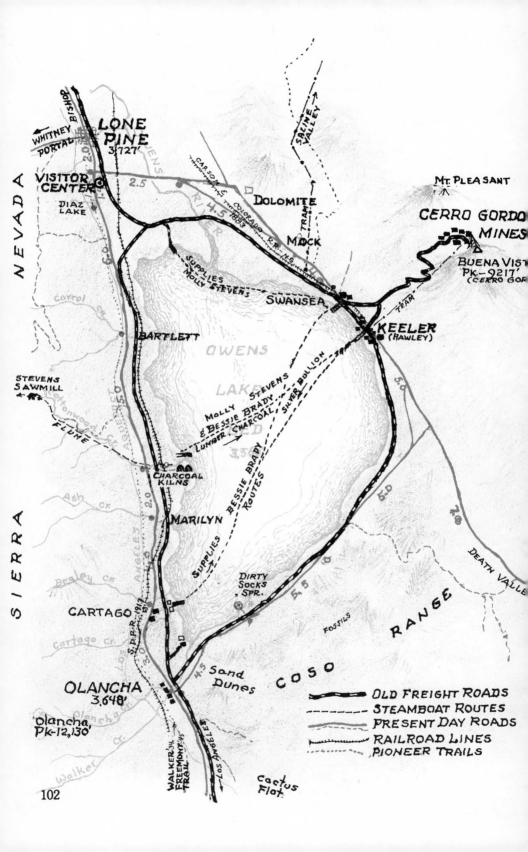

NEVADA

WHITNEY PORTAL

BISHOP

LONE PINE
3,727'

VISITOR CENTER

DIAZ LAKE

Corral

DOLOMITE

CARSON & COLORADO R.R. N.G. 1883

MACK

SALINE VALLEY

TRAM

Mt. PLEASANT

CERRO GORDO MINES

BUENA VISTA
PK-9217'
(CERRO GOR

SUPPLIES
MOLLY STEVENS

BARTLETT

SWANSEA

KEELER
(HAWLEY)

TRAM

OWENS

LAKE

STEVENS SAWMILL

FLUME

Cottonwood Cr.

DRY
3,569'

Molly Stevens
& Bessie Brady
Lumber, Charcoal
Silver Bullion

SIERRA

CHARCOAL KILNS

Ash Cr.

MARILYN

Braley Cr.

SUPPLIES BESSIE BRADY
ROUTES

DIRTY SOCKS SPR.

5.5

5.0

DEATH VALLE

RANGE

COSO

CARTAGO

S.P.R.R. 1917

Cartago Cr.

FOSSILS

2.0

OLANCHA
3,648'

Olancha,
Pk-12,130'

Walker

4.5 Sand Dunes

WALKER & FREEMONT'S TRAIL

LOS ANGELES

Cactus Flat

▬▬▬▬	OLD FREIGHT ROADS
------	STEAMBOAT ROUTES
▬▬▬▬	PRESENT DAY ROADS
┼┼┼┼	RAILROAD LINES
·-·-·-	PIONEER TRAILS

102

LOWER OWENS VALLEY

Today's visitors to the Owens Lake area could well spend a week exploring the many evidences of bygone days. Campgrounds are located at Dirty Socks Hot Springs east of Olancha and at Lone Pine. A few people still live at Keeler and Swansea. The old railroad depot, parts of the tramway and an historical monument reminds us of earlier days. The only serious mining today is for the soft ores of Owens Lakebed. The most likely time of the year for a stay here is in spring or fall. Alkaline dust and sand ride on the high winds during late spring and summer.

After passing through the Redrock Canyon area the road parallels the Indian Wells Valley desert region. At Freeman Junction Hwy. 178 leads west to Bakersfield via the Walker Pass and Kern River.

To the northeast of *RIDGECREST* at China Lake, the desert is closed to visitors as it is a testing ground for military purposes. The area includes many points of interest and some old mines as well as Indian sites. Early history, desert ecology and information is available at the Maturango Desert Museum.

NINE-MILE CANYON road leads west and up the South Fork of the Kern River. It is the closest road on the east side to the Domeland Wilderness Area. At Chimney Creek Campground, the Pacific Crest Trail goes north along the crest of the Sierra to the Golden Trout Wilderness.

Around *LITTLE LAKE* the old volcanic flow presents an interesting contrast to the granite hills to the west and the vast Mojave Desert to the south. Red cinder blowouts and ancient black ridges of lava are visible near the road. Fossil Falls can be reached by turning off the highway about two miles north of Little Lake and following the dirt road, turning right after about a half mile. The slick potholes, lava—once hot molten, now cooled in solidified foam, pumice and red cinders are fascinating to explore.

Five Singers, Mt. Owens, Calif.   Francile Hansen

OWENS LAKE

The Owens Lake basin, once a part of the interconnected fresh water lakes of the last ice age, is now a playa or dry, salt covered flat. Since most of the waters of the east Sierra and the Owens Valley have been included into the Los Angeles water management system little water, if any, ever reaches the Owens lakebed. In December of 1977 a visitor to its western shores of Cartago could have visualized what the valley looked like a century ago. Prolonged heavy rains had filled the basin. Water was flowing down the steep, east face of the Sierra and the desert winds drove the lake waters before them like the great waves of yesteryear. It was easy to reconstruct those times when ...

> great stacks of silver bars were piled like cordwood near the lake's edge. In midlake a steamer's whistle announced its pending arrival loaded with more bullion brought down from the Cerro Gordo mine located high on the slopes of Buena Vista Peak....

Though loaded to dangerous capacity in such rough waters it still could not keep pace with the accumulation of silver bullion bars at the Keeler dock. Daily, several wagon loads were engineered down the steep mountain via the Old Yellow Grade Road. Smelters, near the mine and also on the flat between the lake and the abrupt mountain, worked continuously to reduce the crude ores to more manageable bars for shipping. As steamers returned to the east shore they were loaded with supplies from Los Angeles and lumber cut from the nearby Sierra hills to shore up the mine shafts and erect buildings in the mining town.

To the west at the Cartago landing teamsters, swampers, and blacksmiths worked almost the clock around to keep the precious freight moving. As many as eighty long-line outfits were on the road at one time. In Los Angeles it became an almost unnoticed hourly event for a team to rumble through town delivering another load of silver ingots to the wharf where ships waited to move them to San Francisco for refining.

Around the north end of the lake teams hauled produce from the Owens Valley ranches and lumber cut from the higher shoulders of Cottonwood Creek. Lumber arrived at the loading platforms wet from the flume waters that has slushed them down the canyon from the sawmill. In the early spring and summer months the sandstorms and clouds of alkali dust made this three-day haul a harrowing experience. In winter it was freezing cold from Sierra blasts and in summer the heat was almost intolerable but still the activity went on until the pay given the miners began to amount to more than the pay-dirt taken from the mines.

Cottonwood Charcoal Kilns

Artesian Hot Springs with Olancha Peak in the Background

DIRTY SOCKS MINERAL HOT SPRINGS (4.5 miles east of Olancha; 9.5 miles southwest of Hwy. 190)

Located at the extreme southeast side of Owens lakebed to Death Valley, it offers an interesting rest stop with magnificent views of the surrounding mountains. It makes a good overnight stop for those intending to explore the fossiliferous beds to the southeast between Red Ridge and Sugar Loaf. There is a large, cement-lined pool of warm, saline water. It is fed from a deep-well drilled in 1917 which produced nothing commercially valuable and was abandoned. Some twenty years later an effort was made to develop it as a health spa but this venture met the same fate and all the buildings were removed leaving only the name "Dirty Socks Mineral Hot Springs". How it came by such a name is a matter of conjecture. Some say the odor is from the prospectors who had washed their old socks out here or perhaps it is really submerged minerals brought to the surface by artesian fed waters. It depends on who is telling the story.

ANIMALS IN THE COSOS

The barren tumbled hills of the Coso Range are made up primarily of non-marine sedimentary materials. They have held few promises to prospectors seeking the hardrock ores. But the desert country is full of surprises! No precious metals—but wild animals! Horses and long-tined mastodons! According to paleontologists they were here not too long ago, only about one million years past. These fossil beds, lying east of the highway across from Dirty Socks Hot Springs, were discovered about 1930. Extensive exploratory trips have been made by the California Institute of Technology. Studies have revealed several widely separated fossil areas located in remote ravines. Only a short section of the route can be made by car, and that by a 4x4 drive. The rest is impassable except on foot. It is a three-mile hike and should be undertaken only by those of good purpose in top physical condition who know the dangers of desert cross-country ventures, and are well equipped.

CERRO GORDO

A Mexican prospector, Pablo Floras in 1865 discovered and worked a silver claim near the 8500' level of Buena Vista Peak. From the beginning the operation was very low-key. Crude methods of mining did not accommodate any other way. Lack of water, the curse of all desert mining, prevented much expansion. Water had to be packed in cans by burros for miles. Crude smelting methods required wood carried up the mountain in the same manner. Even though it was recognized as a rich deposit (Cerro Gordo in Spanish means "fat hill"—fat in silver) Mexican "manana" held down development. It might well have become another Lost Burro Mine legend except for an historical turn of events.

The Civil War was closing—many of the men released from the war feared little reward in returning to their homes and pushed west to begin again. Then, in 1866 one Jose Ochoa working the San Lucas Mine, began shipping ore by pack animals to a mill near Independence. Its richness soon attracted the attention of a Fort Independence merchant, Victor Beaudry. He moved to Cerro Gordo, opened a store, and began acquiring some claims. He soon interested outside capital from San Francisco to join in developing the mine. In its early state it became the old badger game of infiltration of the ownership, freeze-out, cutthroat competition between mine owners, transportation units, and merchants.

The chronological story of the Cerro Gordo starts in 1865 when Pablo Floras discovered silver.

1866: Lone Pine Mining District formed. Victor Beaudry opened his store in Cerro Gordo. Financial support from San Francisco expanded activities. A steep toll road was built down eight miles to Owens lakeshore called the Old Yellow Grade Road.

1868: First load of crudely refined silver arrived in Los Angeles. Mortimer Belshaw arrived in Cerro Gordo. He took ore to San Francisco to seek capital to develop mines. Regular shipments of bullion were made to Los Angeles as smelters were built on northeast shore of Owens Lake.

OWENS LAKE
SILVER-LEAD FURNACE

THE OWENS LAKE SILVER-LEAD FURNACE AND MILL WAS BUILT HERE BY COL. SHERMAN STEVENS IN 1869 AND USED UNTIL MARCH 1874. JAMES BRADY ASSUMED ITS OPERATION IN 1870 FOR THE SILVER-LEAD COMPANY AND BUILT THE TOWN OF SWANSEA. DURING THE NEXT FEW YEARS THE OUTPUT OF THIS FURNACE AND ANOTHER AT CERRO GORDO WAS AROUND 150 BARS OF SILVER EVERY 24 HOURS, EACH WEIGHING 83 POUNDS.

CALIFORNIA REGISTERED
HISTORICAL LANDMARK NO. 752

PLAQUE PLACED BY THE CALIFORNIA STATE PARK COMMISSION IN COOPERATION WITH THE EASTERN CALIFORNIA MUSEUM ASSOCIATION, NOVEMBER 5, 1961.

1869: Belshaw introduced the blast furnace ore processing method. Remi Nadeau began his freighting operations to Los Angeles on a large scale hauling 340 tons of bullion. Town had 1500 people with about 1000 claims scattered over the mountain. Owens Lake Silver-Lead Company built a smelter at Swansea.

The three most important mines were Santa Maria, San Felipe and the Union. Los Angeles grew from the needs of the town and business of the mines. San Fernando Valley farmers sold sugar, potatoes, nuts, fruit and barley to the freighters and miners.

1870: Pipeline for water built into Cerro Gordo for ample water. Belshaw & Beaudry produced nine tons of ore per day.

1871: Real mining town in action! Miners lived in tents, caves, rockwall windbreakers, a few in cabins. Excesses in lawless exuberance as it was a wide-open town. Two stages went daily from Owens Valley to the mines. American Hotel and other buildings were erected. Yearly output: 2200 tons, with lead and zinc processed as well as silver. Belshaw controlled two of the three smelters, operated the water supply and owned the toll road—everything but the Owens Lake Silver-Lead Company, which he tried to freeze out.

James Brady was offered Nadeau's freighting contract which expired.

1872: Earthquake in Owens Valley with 27 persons killed in Lone Pine. Little damage at the mines. Floor of the valley under Owens Lake tilted until its waters covered the road along the west shore while they receded along the east side so far the wharves had to be extended!

The Owens Lake Steam Navigation Company was formed. Steamboat *Bessie Brady* built by James Brady was completed. First load of silver bullion out of Swansea crossed in May. This saved some fifty miles freight wagon hauling around the south end of the lake which took four or five days. The west slope landing three miles north of Olancha referred to as Dante's Landing was changed to Cartago.

New problems! Almost a million dollars in bullion was stacked up at Swansea and Cartago landings awaiting shipping. More freighting to Los Angeles had to be done.

1873: Freighting improved by Remi Nadeau, with Beaudry and Belshaw forming the Cerro Gordo Freighting Company. It was a ten day trip over some 225 miles to Los Angeles. Stations were set up a day's haul apart for feed, water and blacksmiths to shoe horses and repair wagons. Redrock Canyon was a busy place as by late summer more than fifty teams were on the road between the north and south terminals, each wagon carrying ten tons of silver bullion. Seven hundred tons per month was moved. Good stock was scarce and demanded high prices all over the west.

Colonel Stevens built a sawmill in June at the head of Cottonwood Canyon near Horseshoe Meadows. Oxen dragged the logs to the mill. From there it was carried by a flume down the steep canyon twelve miles to the loading area where the steamer and teams could haul the timber, charcoal and fuel to the mines.

Belshaw built a new landing on Owens Lake at Keeler, south of Swansea where the Old Yellow Grade Road turned north.

Cottonwood Mill

Bessie Brady

1874: Again water became scarce. Cerro Gordo Water and Mining Company built pipe-lines from Miller Springs in the Saline Valley side of Inyo Mountains and charged three cents per gallon. Three pumps lifted the water over the mountains down into the city. Output now was 400 bars per day. Nadeau delivered more than $4 million worth of silver to Los Angeles. Cerro Gordo was to Los Angeles what the Comstock Lode at Virginia City was to San Francisco in its providing huge sums of capital necessary for its growth.

The Owens Lake Silver-Lead Company at Swansea was closed and a few months later the town was almost buried in a cloudburst-triggered landslide. It never recovered.

1875: Activity starting at Darwin and in the Coso mines. Miners started drifting there.

1876: Belshaw's furnace shuts down. The Union Consolidated Company was formed. The Cottonwood Mills were expanded and the charcoal kilns built inland near the wharves.

1877: The first trip of the *Molly Stevens* steamboat. It served little more than a year. Fire destroyed the Union Mine Mill and some of the shafts.

(Bodie was beginning and was to be a booming mining town by 1881.)

1878: Intense rivalry between the mine operators as law suits increased. Mines began to shut down.

The last stage coach went down the Old Yellow Grade Road.

1879: Zinc discovered. Julius Keeler started laying out his town Hawley near the Cerro Gordo Landing (name later changed to "Keeler"). He reactivated the Union Consolidated Mines as well as Colonel Stevens' lumber operations. *Molly Stevens* was restored and the sawmill was started up again.

1881: Mill at Keeler was completed to process low-grade ore from the mines.

1882: *Molly Stevens* was not too efficient and was dismantled, with its engine refitted into the *Bessie Brady.*

Bessie Brady burned. Steamboat days on Owens Lake were gone.

1883: The Carson & Colorado Railroad came to Keeler. With steamboats and freighting over, Remi Nadeau moved to Arizona.

1883- Long period of inactivity at Cerro Gordo. Became a deserted place except for hand-
1906- ful of hopefuls poking around amid the ruins of another day. Carson & Colorado sold to Southern Pacific.

(Gold was discovered at Tonopah and Goldfield.)

1906: Great Western Ore and Reduction Company begins mining for zinc.

1907: An aerial tramway transported some 50 tons a day from the mines. Became the major source of high grade zinc in the United States.

1909: "Four Metals" Company formed. Once more Keeler stacked bullion bars at its depots.

From Mound House, Nevada, narrow gauge rails of the Carson & Colorado Railroad reached this site in 1883. Cerro Gordo and other mines faltered, the rail line fell on hard times, so plans to extend the line to Mojave were abandoned, leaving Keeler as "End of the Line".

109

1910:   Standard gauge of Southern Pacific Railroad was completed from Mojave to Owens Valley running along west side of Owens Lake, then east to junction with the narrow gauge at Owenyo.

1911:   New zinc discoveries. Tram built down to railroad siding.

1913:   Completion of the Los Angeles Aqueduct. Waters of Sierra flowed into Los Angeles not Owens Lake. Owens Lake had lost its steamboats and now lost its water.
        Revival started at Cerro Gordo as higher prices for metals encouraged reworking old smelters for zinc and silver.

1916:   Electric power came with improvements in mining equipment which led to more extensive explorations with some returns with new investments.

1919:   Tramways carried 16 tons per hour from revival efforts.

1920-   Limestone brought down the tramway to Keeler, with total returns more than $17
1930:   million.

1933-   Several exploratory ventures with no great results, but some zinc still taken
1936:   out.

The great silver days were over. The cool ashes from the fires in the furnaces and kilns have blown away. The railroad tracks have been pulled out. The lake is dry. The steamers are but historical notations in books and models in a museum. The large tailing dumps left up in the mountain and the ghost town rubble of broken glass and rusty tins amid the weather-broken walls are reminders of those great days of the Cerro Gordo. Although it left no city standing with boardwalks and memorabilia, as Virginia City, to commemorate its existence, it was the greatest silver and lead producer in California.

The Comstock and Cerro Gordo marked the poles of the mining world in the west, providing the capital for the development of the "City by the Golden Gate" in the north and the "City of Angels" in the south. Thousands of prospectors who had missed it at these two big ones reasoned that somewhere in the remote ranges of this southwest Basin and Range Country lay another Gold Hill or Silver Queen. Hardly a gully, canyon or rocky ridge escaped their inspection. As years passed prospecting became a way of life. To many, like Pete Auguereberry, Shorty Harris, Ed Teagle and Carl Mengel it became their home. Some lived out their days on their claims working them only enough to make a living. Whereas large operators of the big mines made their money and moved away to the cities.

Swansea Ruins

DARWIN

A decade of activity at Cerro Gordo had left little for other prospectors there. Newcomers pressing on eastward scattered through the Coso Mountains, Santa Rosa Hills and Argus Range. It was a desolate, forbidding land where the ranges ran the wrong way and the streams ran nowhere! Volcanic and sedimentary rocks were intermingled with marble, limestone, and shale in wild confusion. The upturned and folded layers of rocks presented a rough, uninviting landscape. Neither soil nor precipitation encouraged forest cover except at higher elevations. The basin flats contained sparce patches of saltbush. In the washes and higher fans, cactus and cresote bush provided scant coverage to the rubbled debris of cloud-bursts. On a few higher open flats the awkward formed joshua trees stood like abandoned prehistoric creatures waiting in supplication to the heavens to rescue them from such a forsaken place. Today's deserted desert graveyards tell us of only a few who lived out their time in there. The others lay among the lonely hills until the desert heat and sandy winds intermingled their remains with the landscape.

Darwin Schoolhouse Built in 1876

Those who searched for gold found little to satisfy them. However, in 1861 some French prospectors discovered gold in the Coso Range. Mexican, French and American miners joined to make up the lively town of Coso. This ghost town is now closed to the public as it lies within the Naval Weapons Center Range.

In 1874 oxidized silver-lead ore deposits were found in the Darwin Hills which soon led to extensive activity. Most of it was near-surface material producing good returns up to 1880 at a moderate investment by the miners. Within a couple of years smelters at The Defiance, the New Case, and the Cuervo were processing nearly 200 tons a day. Darwin quickly grew to a population of about 1000 people. It was a real mining city of saloons, dance hall girls (from Cerro Gordo), smelters, business opportunists, claim jumpers, and like other mining towns it was for a time a rough-and-ready place. Water to Darwin and its mining operations was secured via an eight mile pipeline from a spring in the Coso hills. By 1883 more than $2 million dollars had been realized.

After the first easily mined ore was exhausted production slowed. As new strikes at Bodie and Mammoth became known the exodus started. For the next twenty years most of the mines lay dormant or were operated on a reduced scale by a succession of speculative mining operators who spent almost as much on leases, court costs and development as they realized from the mines.

The most profitable among the deposits mined have been lead-silver-zinc, tungsten, antimony, copper, gold and talc. Lead, silver, and copper led in the early years but since 1940 principal production has been in tungsten talc and silver. The total production of the Darwin group of mines has approached $35-40 million of which the largest part was made after 1945.

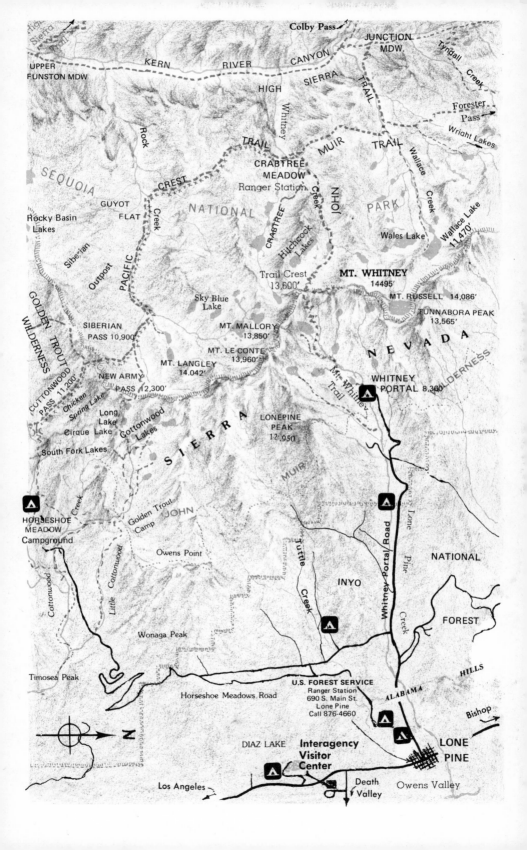

Mt. Whitney Crest

MT. WHITNEY (14,495'): From the Whitney Portal, some thirteen miles west of Lone Pine, the summit can be reached by an excellent Forest Service 10.5 mile trail. The views are tremendous of the entire upper Kern River basin to the west, to the east over the lower Owens Valley and Inyo Mountains, and Basin Ranges to Telescope Peak that overlooks Death Valley. Nearby, along the Whitney Crest are more than a half dozen peaks exceeding 14,000'. At Trail Crest (13,600') the Whitney Trail junctions with the famous John Muir Trail extending north to Yosemite and the High Sierra Trail going west over the Great Western Divide to Giant Forest in Sequoia National Park. This route also connects with the Pacific Crest Trail which extends south to the Mexican border and north to Canada. A quota of 75 persons per day applies to the Mt. Whitney Trail.

LONE PINE

For more than a hundred years the community of Lone Pine has been the gateway to the desert mining country to the west as well as the gathering and outfitting place for the southern Sierra. With the recreational opportunities of fishing, hiking, backpacking to the east, and rock hounding, and ghost town exploring in the mountains and the desert to the east, it is as much a center now as it was with the many miners, prospectors, promoters and ranchers of yesterday.

In early days thousands of sheep were driven through the valley from the upper Kern on their way to Mono Lake and the Bodie Hills for summer grazing. Most of them were driven via trails along the base of the White Mountains. Farmers raised large quantities of hay for the stock used by the long-line teams of Remi Nadeau and other freighters during the mining booms. Tons of fruit from the orchards and vegetables from the truck farms supplemented the diet of bacon and beans of the miners at Cerro Gordo, Darwin, Candelaria and Montgomery. Water from the east Sierra slopes was abundant in those days when the valley flourished with hundreds of small farm homesteads.

In 1904 Los Angeles began using the waters of Owens River for its needs. By 1907 the first portion of the aqueduct was completed. A decade later the valley still produced corn, wheat, potatoes, alfalfa, and grapes. However, in 1921 another drought in the expanding Los Angeles area made it necessary for them to acquire more water rights. Farms were bought up by Los Angeles interests. Water was pumped into the aqueduct and farms faded from the once fertile valley. With the disappearance of the mining towns, and the water supply going to Los Angeles, the people of the valley no longer were supported by ranching and farming. The green of their valley today is the recreation money of the millions of year-round visitors. Tourism has become the foundation of the economic welfare between Lone Pine and Bridgeport.

The new Interagency Visitor Center, one mile south of Lone Pine at Hwy. 190 junction provides extensive information with some dozen federal, state, and local agencies of the eastern California region extending from Death Valley to Topaz Lake, north of Bridgeport. Indoor and outdoor exhibits, large selection of books and maps are available with the latest weather, trail and road conditions.

HORSESHOE MEADOWS (10,000'): Eastern entry point to the new Golden Trout Wilderness, the upper Kern plateau, and the Cottonwood Lakes country. Approach is via the new extension of the Carroll Creek Road west of town. With exceptional scenery in this entire mountain region, trails lead to the Cottonwood Lakes to the north, over Cottonwood Pass to the west, and Trail and Mulkey passes to the south. There are restrictions on some of the Cottonwood Lakes. Check with the Interagency Center or Forest Service before planning a fishing trip to them.

The Golden Trout is California's state fish. Native to the Upper Kern River and Golden Trout Creek, it has since been transplanted to other parts of the Sierra. They interbreed with the rainbow trout producing a wide variety of hybrids from almost golden to almost rainbow. The Mt. Whitney Fish Hatchery, just north of Independence, rears Goldens from brood stocks in the Cottonwood Lakes. These fingerlings are then transplanted by air into suitable waters.

115

ALABAMA HILLS RECREATION AREA with its dramatic High Sierra backdrop, presents an impressive gateway to the Mt. Whitney region. These sculptured rocks of unusual appearance were formed by the same uplifting action as the Sierra over one hundred million years ago. Because of the different rock materials from the granite of the Sierra, these hills have been weathered into their present colorful, rounded shape. Since early days they have been the "movie-lot" for many great western movies. Good roads lead to excellent photographic and picnic sites. For a good loop trip through the hills, just follow the signs for Alabama Hills Scenic Route and Movie Road.

OTHER POINTS OF INTEREST NEARBY: The fault scarp of the 1872 earthquake and the cemetery north of town where the twenty-nine persons who lost their lives then now rest in peace. About ten miles north of Lone Pine on Hwy. 395 is Manzanar, the site of the Japanese relocation camp during World War II. Some 10,000 Japanese-Americans were camped there. The deserted entry gate and few existing concrete foundations are a mute testimony to the spirit of fear this country felt in those years following Pearl Harbor.

For an impressive sweep of the Sierra Crest and a different loop trip to ghost towns and old mining activity in the southern Inyo Mountains, start at the Manzanar Reward Road. Go east across the Owens River to the dirt road south which follows the old roadbed of the narrow gauge to Owenyo. It is now only a site of what once was an active railroad stop and farm community. For an extended trip go south past the Dolomite Hills to Owens Lake before going west to Lone Pine.

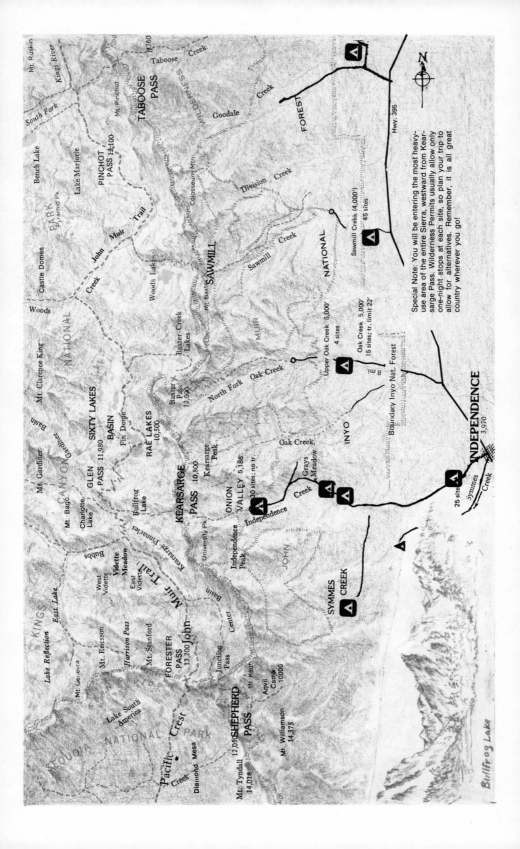

Special Note: You will be entering the most heavy-use area of the entire Sierra, westward from Kearsarge Pass. Wilderness Permits usually allow only one-night stops at each site, so plan your trip to allow for alternatives. Remember, it is all great country wherever you go!

Sierra Panorama—L: Onion Valley, Little Onion Valley; R: No. Fk. Oak Creek   Rocky Rockwell

INDEPENDENCE is the Inyo County seat with a courthouse and free public library with excellent reference materials on desert life and Owens Valley history. The Eastern California Museum has good outdoor and extensive indoor historical exhibits of Indian life, old mining days and early Eastern California memorabilia.

The Commander's House in the center of town was once on the base at Camp Independence. This eastern style, stately structure was built in 1872 to replace the camp's adobe buildings demolished by the earthquake. After the camp was abandoned in 1877 the house was moved into town. Visitors can view the interior on Friday through Tuesday from ten to four.

There are several other historical buildings: the Mary Austin Home and Camp Independence Hospital Building but they are not open to the public. The present courthouse was built in 1921.

Entry into the John Muir Trail country can be made at: Symmes Creek and Shepherd Pass—shortest route to the upper Kern; Onion Valley and Kearsarge Pass—most traveled eastern route to the popular Rae Lakes and Kings River Basin; Oak Creek and Baxter Pass to the Baxter Lakes and Woods Creek country; and Sawmill Creek and Sawmill Pass to Woods Lake and upper Kings River country. All of these backcountry trails into the heart of the High Sierra include the climax of spectacular scenery. With its heavy use, it has necessitated the adoption of entry and use quotas. Wilderness Permits are required and must be secured before entering the John Muir Wilderness. Special precautions regarding the security of your parked car should be observed before leaving on overnight trips.

For a day trip the road up to Onion Valley is most interesting. Usually from late spring until well into summer the visitor will find an extensive presentation of wildflowers. The change from a desert sage environment to juniper forest marks the climatic differences in plant life of the eastern Sierra. Kearsarge Pass, four miles from the roadend at Onion Valley, is the lowest and easiest pass of the southern Sierra. It was used by the Indians to cross to and from the Kings River basin to the west.

118

Although gold quartz was found on the shoulder of Kearsarge Peak and much money was invested in the Kearsarge Mine and mill to process its ore, it never developed as a paying operation and soon folded. Today, little remains among the rocks and brush of the project.

Southeast of Independence along the western front of the Inyo Mountains veins of gold were discovered in 1878 and worked steadily until 1914. The Reward or Brown Monster group of mines provided the largest source of gold. Later, during the 1930's and 1940's the Reward was again active. Moderate amounts of lead, silver, and copper have also been produced.

East of Independence in the Mazourka Canyon dry placer methods were used between 1894 and 1906 to secure free gold. Again, during the depression years of the 30's, the old mine tailings were reworked. The Blue Bell Mine was one of the most productive. A 4 x 4 drive is advised for trips into this area. A journey to the canyon is most rewarding in the spring when wildflowers are at their best and the views of the snow-capped Sierra are magnificent. The site of Kearsarge has been reduced to only scattered bricks along the old Carson & Colorado railroad bed.

CAMP INDEPENDENCE: Three miles north of Independence is the Historical site where the camp was established on Independence Day, 1862, to quelch the Indian disturbances against miners and settlers in Owens Valley. Supplies were brought in from Visalia for the 200 men stationed here via the old Hockett Trail across the Kern Plateau.

FISH REARING: The Mt. Whitney Fish Hatchery is located four miles north of town on the North Fork of Oak Creek. More than four million fingerling trout are raised there each year, which are then planted in lakes and streams of the eastern Sierra. The Blackrock Rearing Ponds produce more than a half million catchable-size trout each year, with some 100,000 subcatchables nurtured for the following year. West of Tinemaha Reservoir at Fish Springs Fish Hatchery more than one and a half million catchable trout are raised each season. All of these operations are open daily to visitors.

TULE ELK VIEWPOINT: Just east of Hwy. 395 is the reserve that maintains a refuge for a species of Tule Elk found only here and in Colusa County. Their ancestors formerly roamed in great herds in California's Central Valley. Early morning and late afternoon are the most likely times for seeing them.

BIGHORN SHEEP ZOOLOGICAL AREAS: Once, very common in high mountains and desert plateaus of the west, they are now quite rare. Several special areas protecting the Bighorn Sheep have been set aside such as those near Mt. Williamson and Mt. Baxter where specific limitations of travel are enforced in an effort to stabilize the size and well-being of their bands.

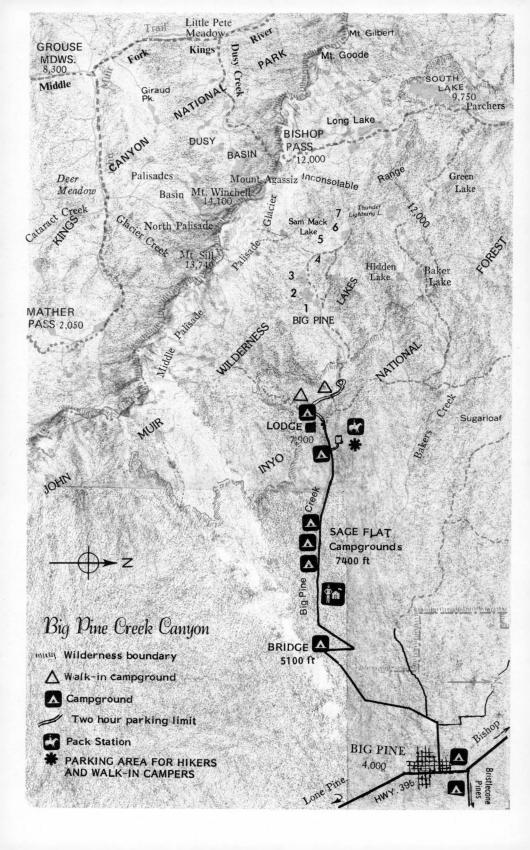

Middle Palisade Glacier   Rocky Rockwell

BIG PINE is twice blessed with wonders of the mountains. To the west, nestled against the craggy peaks of the Palisade Crest, is the largest and most southern of more than three score glaciers of the Sierra Nevada. To the east in the White Mountains is the Ancient Bristlecone Pine Forest.

The Palisade Glacier between Mt. Sill and Mt. Winchell, covering almost a square mile, moves downward some forty feet per year. The milky-green water of the glacial lakes below is evidence of this movement. Originally it extended down Big Pine Creek Canyon to the 5000' level. It is seven miles from the roadend and almost a mile higher in elevation. Access to the foot of the glacier is by trail only past Sam Mack Lake. A two-day trip should be planned by hikers.

Both glacier and rock climbing in conditions such as these found in the Palisades should be attempted only by the experienced. This area lies within the John Muir Wilderness and permits are required. Updated information is available where they are issued. This precipitous front wall of the Sierra holds no encouragement for the building of trails across it. The only trail in the canyon leads to the seven Big Pine Lakes group and the one going north to South Lake.

121

Tramway and Salt Flats of Saline Valley

About 2.5 miles east of Big Pine the Devils Gate road branches. Each leads to some interesting mining country and eventually to Saline or Eureka valleys. Notable among these were the mines on the north and east shoulders of Andrews Mountain. These are found in Marble Canyon and several canyons on the south eastern slope of the Inyo Mountains. They produced gold, silver, zinc, lead, soda, manganese, talc, and tungsten. Visitors equipped for a long backcountry desert trip can continue this Devils Gate-Saline Valley road south through the Santa Rosa Hills to junction with Hwy. 190 just north of the Darwin area.

The north fork of Devils Gate Road leads to Eureka Valley via Little Cowhorn Valley and Joshua Flats. It continues southeast across Eureka Valley, through the Last Chance Range and Sand Spring to Death Valley National Monument.

Saline Valley   Rocky Rockwell

WESTGARD PASS ROAD (Hwy. 168): This route to the Bristlecone Pine Forests and western Nevada has an interesting place in the early history of the region. The depression in the range between Big Pine and the eastern desert provided the crossing of the White-Inyo Mountains by Indians, soldiers, and prospectors. A rough road opened by the Camp Independence soldiers was referred to as the Old South Trail. With increased discoveries of gold in the Deep Srpings Valley and the Waucoba area, the Deep Springs Mining District was established. Early assays were encouraging. A stamp mill was built at White Mountain City just west of Gilbert Pass. It soon became apparent that the road would not be adequate and steps were taken to build a better one. Private interests constructed the Toll Road. After White Mountain City faded, following the course of many early mining ventures, the Deep Springs Toll Road was taken over by the County road department. At one time support was given to develop this route as a main highway between Owens Valley and Goldfield. It became known as Westgard Pass Road in honor of an AAA official who had encouraged a new route. Today, it is a paved, winding highway that provides easy access between Big Pine and Nevada.

DEEP SPRINGS VALLEY-FISH LAKE VALLEY TOUR

In the spring when wildflowers are at their best and weather is mild, a loop trip of the White Mountains offers an interesting view of the desert and the great eastern rampart of the range. This venturesome trip may be made by continuing east on the Westgard Pass Road to Deep Springs Valley. Beyond the maintenance station a road up Wyman Creek one half mile leads to the site of White Mountain City. Very little is left as the mining venture folded before any great amount of development was done. The old sheep corrals, in zig-zag pattern, mark the location where stock was herded. A dirt road follows up Wyman Creek to junction with the Bristlecone road. Seasonal conditions affect its condition. Inquire before attempting it.

At Oasis Ranch turn north on Hwy. 166 through Fish Lake Valley with its fertile alfalfa fields in the shadow of the imposing White Mountains. Junctioning with Hwy. 6 go west over Montgomery Pass. Along this route crossing the mountains can be seen the old grade of the Carson & Colorado Railroad. This trip follows to Benton, south to Bishop and Hwy. 395. The trip is 160 miles. Gas is available at Dyer and Benton.

Rocky Rockwell

"Wind of the East, wind of the West, wandering
to and fro,
Chant your songs in the topmost boughs, that the
sons of men may know
The peerless pine was the first to come, and the
pine will be last to go!"

From THE PINES, by Robert Service

THE ANCIENT BRISTLECONE PINE FOREST

Bristlecone Pine (pinus longaeva)

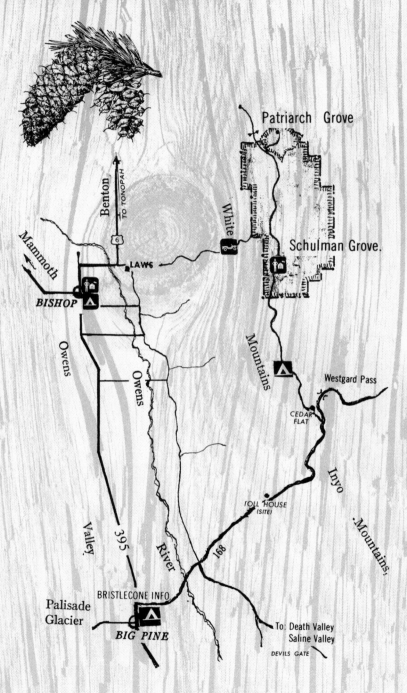

Patriarch Grove

Benton

TO TONOPAH

6

White

Schulman Grove

Mammoth

LAWS

BISHOP

Owens

Mountains

Owens

Westgard Pass

CEDAR
FLAT

Inyo

Owens

Mountains

Valley

395

TOLL HOUSE
(SITE)

River

168

Palisade
Glacier

BRISTLECONE INFO

BIG PINE

To: Death Valley
Saline Valley

DEVILS GATE

Bristlecone Country   Rocky Rockwell

THE ANCIENT BRISTLECONE PINE FOREST

Sheltered by the isolation of the rugged Basin Ranges, the bristlecone pines have, except for a few mining ventures, been by-passed with the inroads of man. Awareness of their existence and significance have developed only in the past few decades. Actually, they are found in six of the southwestern states and, like the hardy Scots, seem to have an affinity to adversity. They grow in scattered, open forest groups on the most desolate high mountains of Colorado's Rockies, and the Basin Ranges of California, Nevada, and Utah. Also, in limited areas of New Mexico and Arizona.

It seems that their perversity in growing where conditions are the most difficult must, in some way, contribute to their ability to survive. Certainly it has aided them in their escape from man's destruction in his intrusion into the western wilderness. Their lifespan on the rugged crests are much longer than of those that grow in more sheltered places where soil and precipitation have been more ample. In the dolomite (limestone) soil of the White Mountains are found the oldest trees. It seems a most fitting phenomenon that earth's oldest living things cling to life with far reaching roots to gather their strength from soils made up from fossil beds of ancient sea life.

In contrast to the massive sequoias of the western Sierra slope and the towering coast redwoods, the bristlecone seldom reach more than 25'-30' tall. When quite young they resemble other small pines, especially the limber pines. Many of them develop great matts of limbs that hug the ground so that winter snows pile up on them sheltering them from ice-laden blasts blowing across from the Sierra.

As the centuries roll by and their upright trunks are blasted by sand and ice storms many of them seek the solace of their youth and survive in great low lying limbs, even when only a narrow strip of living bark is left. When adverse soil and weather conditions begin to overwhelm them, they conserve life by channeling their strength into a single branch or two to compensate for their meager root strength to support it. Many trees grow almost prostrate to the ground; others develop massive multiple trunks and limbs that may reach only 20' to 30' in height.

126

The bark of the old trees is a dull, reddish brown and is shallowly furrowed. The limbs, as well as the trunks, of small trees are smooth and chalky white. Their deep green foliage is densely clustered at the ends of the twig. Needles 1¼″-1½″ long grow in a cluster.

Variations in temperature and precipitation over several decades can be "read" from some small branches. The tree retains the needles for at least ten years—some as long as thirty to forty years. As many as fifty-eight successive needle groups have been counted. The key to this variation lies in the lengths of needle groups—it is closely related to summer temperatures. A short, cold summer results in shorter needles than those produced in a long, warm one. Thus, a study of long term fluctuations in tree growth reflects a seasonal trend in climate. When calibrated with tree-ring widths significant conclusions have been made respecting long-range climatic changes.

It takes up to one hundred years to accumulate one inch of growth rings in the trunk. Narrow rings indicate short, cold summers with little moisture. Sometimes growth stops altogether except in a very narrow strip of bark and then resumes its growth when more favorable conditions return.

The wood from mature limbs and trunk is of a pale brownish red. It is coarse-grained, light, soft, and very brittle. It has been of little economic value save when there was no other wood available some miners used it for shoring in tunnels or shafts.

Ripe cones 2¼″-3¼″ mature at the very top of branches at the end of the second season. They are chocolate brown, with a purplish tinge. The end of each cone scale is tipped with a bristle-like, very fragile prickle. Trees bear cones when they are about twenty years old and seed is produced almost every year thereafter. Some years the seeds are more numerous than others. The seedlings take root most readily some distance from the parent tree.

Rocky Rockwell

A TRIP TO THE BRISTLECONES

Condition of Travel: Usually open from June to October. Total 35 miles one way. This is a remote area, no roadside or commercial services are available. Be sure you are well supplied with gas, water, spare tire, lunch, camera, and film. There is only one campground on the trip at Grandview. (No water, take your own wood, or better, a gas stove.)

The road is paved as far as the Schulman Grove. Beyond there, although dirt, it is well graded. You are going to climb from 4000' at Big Pine to an elevation of more than 10,000' at the Schulman Grove and up to 11,000' at the Patriarch Grove. Cars in reasonably good condition should have no trouble—some may exhibit carburetor disturbance due to the lack of oxygen. Those with trailers and large RV's should not attempt to go further than the Schulman Grove—leave your trailer at Grandview Campground. Auto travel is limited to established roads only. There are some 4 x 4 drive trails not suitable for conventional cars in the White Mountain area. See accompanying map. It could be quite cold at night as well as very windy, especially in early or late season.

The first half of the route follows Highway 168 east—the Westgard Pass Road. A display at the junction with Hwy. 395 tells about the trees. (The large, symmetrical dark green tree nearby is a *sequoia,* normally found on the west slope of the Sierra.) In the early days this Westgard Pass-Deep Springs route was a toll road. The old Toll House station site and spring are some eight miles east.

The road continues up through the Narrows to the Cedar Flat junction (7,000') just below the Westgard Pass (13 miles from Big Pine). During mining days junipers were called cedar, thus this juniper forest is known as Cedar Flat. Highway 168 continues east to Deep Springs (15 miles) and Oasis (25 miles). The White Mountain Road north to the Ancient Bristlecone Pines begins at this junction.

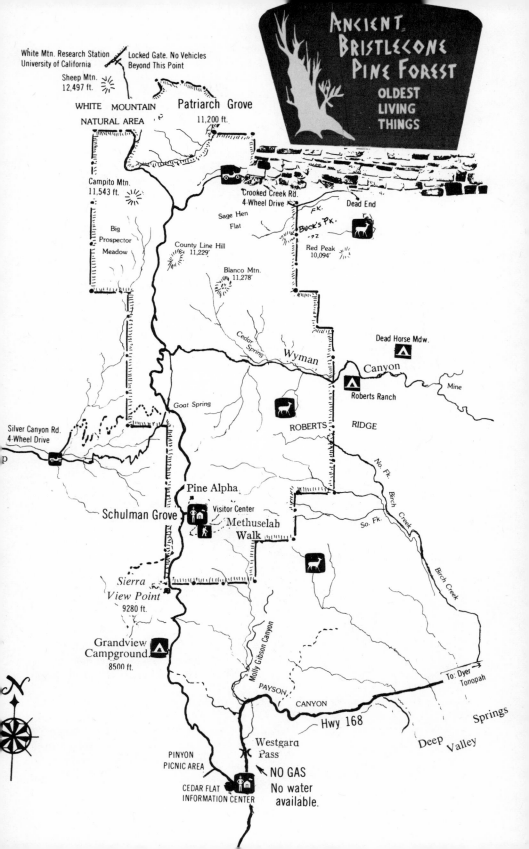

About three and a half miles up is a picnic site (8,000'). In this area, there are coralline fossils from the Lower Cambria Age, some five hundred million years ago. Between Cedar Flat and the southern boundary of the Bristlecone Forest, this undulating plateau supports an extensive forest of pinyon pine and juniper. At the higher elevations these give way to limber pine and bristlecone. Pure stands of the latter are scattered on the highest slopes and ridges.

Grandview Campground (8,200') is quite unique in its setting. Campsites, among the pinyons have tables and iron grate stoves. To camp here in this high pine plateau is a unique mountain experience. After a quiet, clear starlit night take a short walk in the early morning to see the sun glow on the grand sweep of the Sierra rampart.

Sierra View Overlook (9,000') presents a panorama of the Sierra crest extending from south to Mt. Whitney, north to Mt. Dana and other eastern Yosemite peaks near Tioga Pass. Below to the west lies the Owens Valley trench and the city of Bishop. To the southeast, you can look into Deep Springs Valley and over the Basin Ranges to Death Valley. A display indicates important Sierra peaks. A short trail leads south to the Mt. Whitney viewpoint with an exhibit showing geologic contrasts of the Sierra Nevada and the White Mountains.

Rocky Rockwell

Just beyond the Sierra View, you enter the Ancient Bristlecone Pine Forest. At this higher elevation, the limber pines and bristlecone pines can be seen close by. The limber pines grow in sheltered areas, while the bristlecones prefer the open slopes. The lack of underbrush and general arid conditions result in the moisture from the Pacific being lost crossing the Sierra crest and leaving little for the White Mountains and Basin Ranges farther east. The annual precipitation (snow and rain) is less than 12 inches at the Schulman and Patriarch groves. Wildflowers on these rolling highlands can be seen in August. Blue lupine and Indian paintbrush are among the varieties of plants found here. The birds, plants and wildlife are similar to those found in Sierra Nevada in comparable elevation and life zones.

SCHULMAN GROVE (10,000′) is the general activity center for the Bristlecone Forest. In season, a Ranger-Naturalist of the Forest Service conducts small group discussions, suggests what to see and how to appreciate these trees, what to specifically look for when walking through the grove. He is ready to assist in emergencies and there is radio contact with the Owens Valley Forest Service Station. Picnic tables, restrooms and the Visitor Information Center are here for your use (ample parking).

Two easy, self-guided tours enable you to explore on your own. The *Pine Alpha Trail* leads out a half mile to the first tree discovered by Dr. Schulman to be dated older than 4,000 years. The age of the tree was determined by using a Swedish instrument that bores a small cylinder to remove a cross-ring core of annual rings. Interestingly enough, the Pine Alpha has living tissue in less than ten percent of its circumference yet it can still produce viable seeds.

The Methuselah Walk extends for about two miles to include the viewing of trees, many over 4,000 years old. The oldest tree is 4,600 years old— actually living since the time of the Babylonians. Along the walk you'll notice the old trees outnumber the new and young. Twisted trunks and beautiful formed stumps will delight the artist and photographer for the dramatic settings here. (Please stay on the trail when taking pictures.)

The *Limber Pine* also seen in this area can be distinguished from the bristlecone by the short tufts at the end of their branches, while the bristlecone pine needles run back along the branch. Old trunks have bark of dark brown, very aromatic, with deep furrows between wide rectangular blocks. On young trees the bark is thin and smooth and the branches are a bright whitish gray, often silvery. The foliage is dark yellow-green and heavy set at the ends of the branches. The needles are five in a cluster. These pines are also found in the Sierra Nevada.

132

THE PATRIARCH GROVE (11,000') is located twelve miles north of the Schulman Grove. It is at the end of a dirt road, mostly narrow and in a few places one-way. However, it is really very safe if driven with care. The last three miles get rather rough in places with steep pitches up the mountain slope and around some of the bristlecones. It is an exhilarating, adventurous trip, climbing so high with all the surrounding mountains below you. Those driving heavy or long RV's should not attempt it. It is "backcountry" exploratory-type travel. In some places, the road traverses high, open sagebrush covered country where, in season, wildflowers, birds, small animals, and deer are frequently seen. Expansive, alternate views are offered west over the Owens Valley to the massive Sierra crest and east to the Silver Peak Range and Esmeralda mining country of the late 1800's. At the end of the road there is a large area for ample parking.

The Patriarch, the world's largest bristlecone pine, is reached by an easy trail. This pine is about 1500 years old. Its trunk is actually a composite of several units resulting in a circumference of 36' 8". The setting is truly a photographer's paradise. Beauty is found in the minute lines of the old, eroded, weatherbeaten trunks in extreme closeups or of twisted, gnarled limbs silhouetted against great piles of cumulus clouds in the deep blue sky of summer.

The surrounding open forest spreads over the hillside with specimens of unique grandeur. These rugged, barren slopes meet the ultimate in weather conditions—wind, ice and sandstorms. This higher elevation produced larger, more bizarre shaped trees than those found at Schulman Grove.

To the northeast you can look off to the misty valleys below with layers of blue turning to gray mountains in the far off distance. On a clear day you feel as if you can see forever!

Bristlecone pines are intolerant to shade and never form dense stands. They are scattered on slopes where the snow melts early and evaporation is rapid. Except for a direct lightning strike, fires seldom destroy them as there is little or no underbrush to feed a fire.

A 7100-year true chronology has been developed from the bristlecone pine of the White Mountains by the addition of data from long dead wood specimens, from dead standing trees, and from living trees 4,000 years old. With the width of growth rings of trees at higher elevations closely related to temperature changes a valuable guide is provided to determine past climatic circumstances. At White Mountains studies of *dendrochronology,* (the method of using tree rings as a measurement of time and environmental conditions) show that the summers between the years 3500 BC-1300 BC were relatively warm, the years between 1300 BC and 200 BC were cold.

The dirt road branching off to the northwest leads to the White Mountain Scientific Area. Special permits are required for entry. There are several laboratories for research and observation established on the White Mountains. Roads are closed except to authorized personnel.

The U.S. Forest Service, in 1935, set aside 2330 acres which included the Patriarch Grove as the White Mountain Natural Area, a preserve for the bristlecone pine. In 1958, an additional 28,000 acres were added to make up the Ancient Bristlecone Pine Forest as a Botanical Area to be administered for scientific study as well as for public enjoyment.

To assist in preserving this Botanical Area, the U.S. Forest Service has specified that:

1. All wood, dead or living, downed or standing must remain as you find it.
2. There is no overnight camping which includes campers and trailers. It is a day use only area.
3. All vehicles must remain on the established roads.
4. All Indian artifacts must be left where they are for others to see and appreciate.
5. No fires, barbecues, hibachis, etc., are allowed.
6. To collect rock specimens, shrubs or flowers, a special permit must be granted from the Forest Service.

This area is patrolled and the regulations are strictly enforced.

Dr. C.W. Ferguson of University of Arizona, making scientific studies.   Rocky Rockwell

Other significant effects of the studies of these trees have been modifications in the use of radio-carbon (C-14) datings applied to archaeology. This has resulted in a new perspective of the time sequence of ancient European artifacts. Tree-ring calibrations indicate long accepted dates by historians of pre-history Europe may be off as much as 700 years.

Additional scientific studies for research are being carried on at the White Mountain Summit Laboratory (14,246') and the Mt. Bancroft Laboratory (12,500'). This truly is an area where academic concerns match the breadth of the scenic skylines about it.

WHITE MOUNTAIN PEAK (14,246') is the third highest summit in the state of California being exceeded only by Mt. Whitney (14,495') and Mt. Williamson (14,375').

Lassie, Corby Stuart, Rocky Rockwell during the filming of the TV show when   Courtesy of Inyo National Forest
Lassie helped out the Forest Service. Parts of the series were filmed in the White
Mountains.

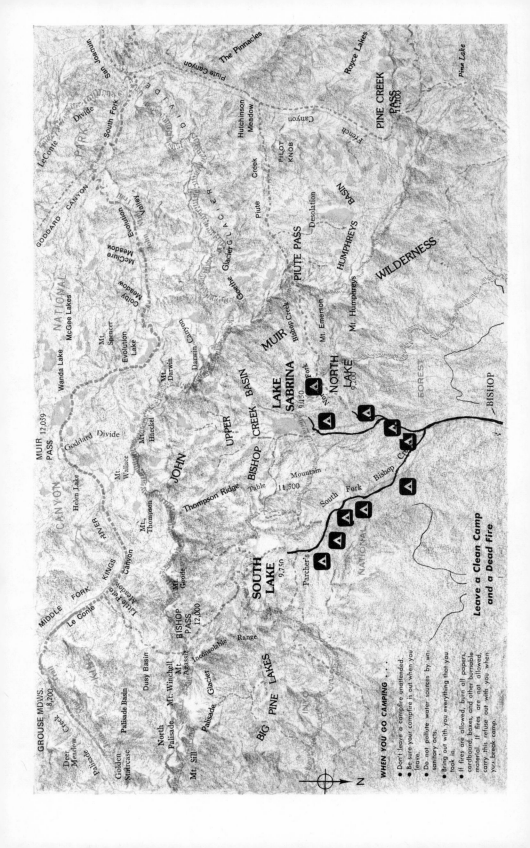

WHEN YOU GO CAMPING . . .

- Don't leave a campfire unattended.
- Be sure your campfire is out when you leave.
- Do not pollute water sources by un-sanitary acts.
- Bring out with you everything that you took in.
- If fires are allowed, burn all papers, cardboard, boxes, and other burnable material. If fires are not allowed, carry this refuse out with you when you break camp.

Leave a Clean Camp and a Dead Fire

Forest Service Office, Bishop circa 1923   Courtesy of Inyo National Forest

MINING IN THE BISHOP AREA

The Bishop-Benton country has been active in mining since the Civil War times. Mines in the upper Bishop Creek canyons produced lead-silver east of South Lake and gold in the Cardinal mine just below Lake Sabrina above Aspendell. Up Coyote Creek some half dozen tungsten mines operated between Lookout Mountain and the Hunchback.

At one time, the Poleta mine supported the town of Owensville. In 1869, Mexicans were mining the one good producing claim. Ores from the Poleta, Black Canyon mines, and the Southern Belle were milled at Owensville. Subsequent owners and miners worked the claim through the years—one even built a mill and had a 3800' pipeline from Redding Canyon bringing water to it.

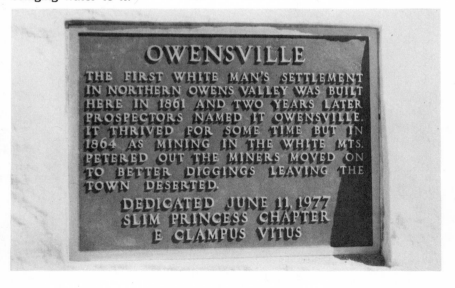

OWENSVILLE

THE FIRST WHITE MAN'S SETTLEMENT IN NORTHERN OWENS VALLEY WAS BUILT HERE IN 1861 AND TWO YEARS LATER PROSPECTORS NAMED IT OWENSVILLE. IT THRIVED FOR SOME TIME BUT IN 1864 AS MINING IN THE WHITE MTS. PETERED OUT THE MINERS MOVED ON TO BETTER DIGGINGS LEAVING THE TOWN DESERTED.

DEDICATED JUNE 11, 1977
SLIM PRINCESS CHAPTER
E CLAMPUS VITUS

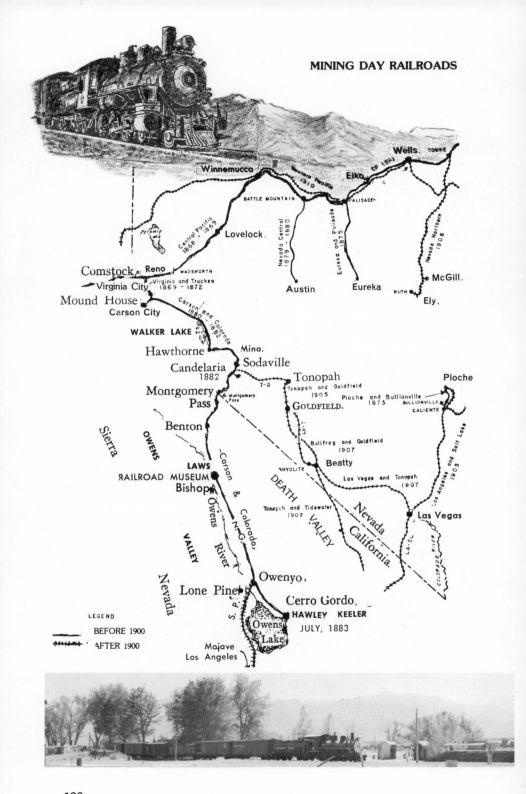

LAWS AND THE SLIM PRINCESS

Cattle and sheep could be driven to railway sidings, even hundreds of miles. But, with the coming of extensive mining to the White-Inyo Range something more was needed—a railroad to run north and south between the transcontinental lines at Reno and Barstow. Born by this necessity it was inevitable that in later years as the mines were worked out, railroading also became a fading venture.

While it lasted, it was the practical answer to that day's needs and gave today's visitor a romantic reminder of the wood-burning narrow-gauge railroad that opened up eastern California and western Nevada. The indoor-outdoor displays at Laws is a touch of yesterday enjoyed by railroad buffs, mining day enthusiasts, and all the kids that climb over the cars and into the cab of old No. 9 to ring the engine bell and make believe they are the engineer bringing a load of freight or gold and silver ore into the station.

The depot, completed in 1883, had a large attic for the workers to sleep in and a large pot-bellied stove that kept the building warm. Lumber for this depot was hauled by team from Mammoth. The town had two boarding houses, pool hall, blacksmith shop, grocery store, school and post office. By 1960 the trains were gone and few people lived in the town. The post office operates a mail route from Bishop to Tonopah, then returns via Westgard Pass and Big Pine.

The Southern Pacific gave the buildings, remaining cars, and engine No. 9 to Inyo County and the City of Bishop in the form of a gift deed. Laws was turned into an indoor-outdoor museum. *NEVADA SMITH* starring Steve McQueen was filmed here. Paramount Studio left buildings they had constructed for the movie and they are now being used to house some of the artifacts.

Upper Bishop Creek

ANGLERS MAP

Adapted from materials provided by
California Department of Fish & Game
U. S. Forest Service

JOHN MUIR TRAIL

Evolution Lake

NEVADA

Wanda Lake

Mt Darwin 13830

Mt Haeckel 13435

Mt Wallace 13377

Blue Heaven Lake 11,850

Hell Diver Lakes 11,750

Schober Hole Lakes

Mt Powell

National Park

Hungry Packer Lake 11,100

Midnight Lake 11,000

Bottleneck Lake 11,200

Fishgut Lakes 11,100

Echo Lake 11,650

Dingleberry Lake 10,500

Emerald Lakes 10,450

Sunset Lake 11,500

Moonlight Lake 11,050

Drunken Sailor 11,000

Topsy Turvy 10,800

Pee Wee 10,800

Mt Thompson 13494

Baboon Lakes 11,000

Donkey Lake 10,600

Blue Lake 10,400

Canyon

RIDGE

Thompson Lake 12,150

THOMPSON

George Lake 10,700

Little George Lake 10,700

JOHN MUIR TRAIL

Kings

Mt Gilbert 13232

Mt Johnson

SIERRA

Treasure Lakes
8 7 6 5 4 3 2 1 10,646

6 11,100
5
4
3
Tyee Lakes 2 10,300
1

SOUTH LAKE

9800

HIKER PARKING

Bishop Pass

Bishop Lake 11,200

Mt Goode 13068

Saddlerock Lake 11,100

Timberline Tarns 11,300

Margaret Lakes 11,050

Spearhead Lake 10,800

Ruwau Lake 10,800

Phyllis Ledge 11,150

Long Lake 10,700

Chocolate Lakes 11,400

Hurd Lake 10,300

Bull Lake 10,750

Inconsolable Lake 10,900

Mary Louise Lakes 10,650

Mule Lake 10,300

Wilderness

PARCHER'S VILLAGE

RAINBOW PACK STATION

9000

Green Lake 11,100

Brown Lake

Bluff Lake 10,500

WILLOW 8800 ft.

South

INCONSOLABLE RANGE

UPPER BISHOP CREEK LAKES

AREA	Miles from Roadend	Size in Acres	Type of Fish	Size of Fish
SOUTH LAKE				
Green Lake	1.4	17.5	RT	14"
Tyee Lake No. 4	2	11	RT	15"
Thompson	5	9.6	EB	12"
Treasure No. 1	2	42	GT	12"
Chocolate No. 1	1.5	1	EB	7"
Long Lake	1.5	29	all	17"
Saddlerock	2	30	RT	10"
Bishop Lake	2.5	25	EB	14"
SABRINA				
George L.	2	12	EB, RT	12"
Blue	1.5	30	EB, RT	16"
Sunset	3.5	29	EB	16"
Topsy Turvy	3	10	EB	8"
Moonlight	4	32	EB	12"
Hungry Packer	4	41	RT	10"
Echo	2	48	EB	10"
NORTH LAKE				
Loch Leven	1.5	10	RT, BN	10"
Upper Lamarck	1.5	15	RT, EB	12"
Piute Lake	2	19	RT, EB	10"

Mt Lamarck 347

Sky High Lake 11,870

Wishbone Lake 11,500

Upper Lamarck Lake 10,950

Lower Lamarck Lake

Wander Lakes 11,100

Emerson Lake 11,200

Piute Lake 10,960

Piute Pass BM 11423

Mt Emerson 13225

Loch Leven

North Fork

John Muir Wilderness

Hutchinson Meadow

FOREST

Scale in Miles 0 1/4 1/2 3/4

SCHOBER PACK STATION

NORTH LAKE 9500 ft. (Walk-In)

NATIONAL

LAKE SABRINA 9130

BOAT RENTALS

Grass Lake 9,900

CREEK

HIKER PARKING

CARDINAL LODGE

BISHOP PARK

BISHOP PARK (GROUP)

INTAKE TWO

Bishop

395

7800 ft.

FORKS

FOUR JEFFREY 3100 ft.

BIG TREES 7500 ft.

MOUNTAIN GLEN (Walk-In) 8400 ft.

Bishop Creek

BISHOP CREEK LODGE

HABEGGER'S RESORT

INYO

MOUNTAIN

BLE

N Fork

Five varieties of trout are found in the 83 lakes in the upper Bishop Creek area: Eastern Book — 58; Rainbow — 36; Golden — 9; Brown — 5; and Kamloops Rainbow — 3. Nearly all of the lakes are less than three hours one way from road ends at South Lake, Lake Sabrina and North Lake. With the exception of these lakes, all are above 10,000' in elevation — 40 are above 11,000' and Thompson Lake is 12,150'.

Rocky Rockwell

BISHOP CREEK BASIN

One-day fishermen and overnight hikers have a lot to choose from in the great basin that includes eighty-three lakes and many miles of streams. Camping facilities vary from full hookups for trailers to walk-in camps and backcountry trips for backpackers and saddle parties. All areas within the John Muir Wilderness require permits even for day use. All but South Lake, Lake Sabrina, and North Lake are above 10,000'. The extensive trail system within the basin is well marked. Exit over the Sierra crest is made at Bishop Pass and Piute Pass. Both of these routes tie in with the John Muir-Pacific Crest Trail to provide a circle trip including the grandeur of Le Conte Canyon, Muir Pass and Evolution Valley.

French Canyon: Steelhead, Moon, Puppet Lakes; Pilot Knob in center   Chuck Koons

PINE CREEK

Pine Creek Canyon is no modest creek-worn ravine. Ancient glaciers carved out its walls in dramatic form and left behind the U-shaped canyon typical of the Kings and Tuolumne river basins. Its middle and upper benches support juniper, limber pine and lodgepoles. The paved road follows close to Pine Creek but is a no-nonsense, steep climb. Parking is limited at roadend so large RV units are not advised.

Trailheads to Pine Creek or Italy passes start near the corral and follow the narrow mining road on the shady side of the canyon to the old Brownstone Mine. Rainbow, brook and goldens are found in the many lakes in the upper basins. The trail over the summit near Morgan Peak leads to Little Lakes Valley on upper Rock Creek. Its trailhead is located at the Muir Wilderness boundary, about four miles up from the mill entrance. Beyond the Union Carbide Mine the road is private and closed to vehicles. Only foot travel is permitted. These routes lead into the famous fishing country of French Canyon, Humphrey's Basin, Lake Italy, the Bear Lakes, and the upper Mono Creek recesses. All tremendous fishing country!

Tungsten with a melting point of 6152° is of vital importance to the manufacture of heat-resistant steel, as well as many other products ranging from wire filaments to armor piercing projectiles. The Union Carbide Corporation at the head of Pine Creek is a major producer of tungsten in the United States today. Copper, gold, molybdenum and scheelite are also processed. The Black Rock Mine in the Benton area is another source of tungsten, which utilizes both open-pit and underground workings.

143

OLD BENTON AND BENTON STATION

Old Benton (now Benton Hot Springs, also once called Warm Springs) was at its peak in the early 1880's when it was the trading center for the Blind Spring Hill Mines as well as others farther north and west. One report indicates that more than 200,000 head of sheep were sheared there each year. With the completion of the Carson & Colorado Railroad to Keeler in 1883, Benton Station became active having a large freight yard at the depot that serviced the ranches, people of the town as well as the many surrounding mines. Tons of machinery, boilers, compressors, animal feed,

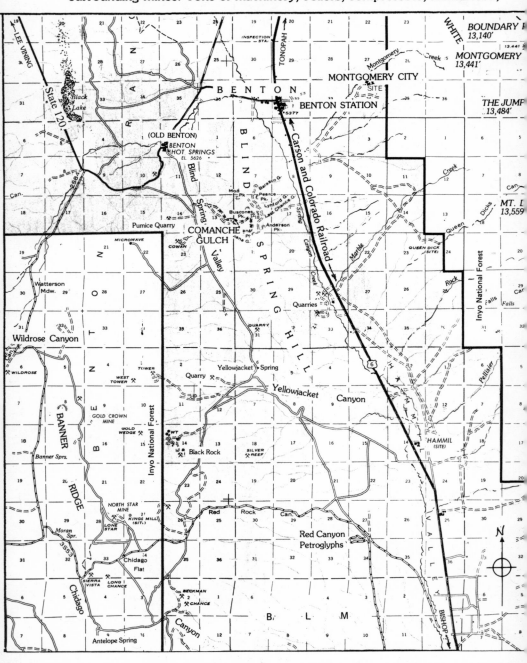

and groceries were unloaded from the trains. In turn, gold, silver, copper, and other ores, cattle, horses, sheep and wool were shipped to San Francisco and points east. Some of the silver from the Benton mining area was used at the Carson City mint to make coins.

East of Benton gold and silver bearing ores were secured from a number of mines in Montgomery Canyon. For a time it looked as though Montgomery City might become more than a "place on a map". Little is left except a few old rock walls, rough timbers, and the scarred hillside diggings where forlorn hope faded. With the passing of a cloudburst flood that wiped out most of the place, the discouraged prospectors moved on. Several other mines along the west slope of the White Mountains failed for lack of good ore.

The Blind Spring Hill mines were more generous than those of Montgomery Canyon. Some $4-$5 million in silver was taken before the ore ran out. Several old mines were developed in Comanche Gulch (as shown on the map). Many of the workers were Chinese or Indian. Although the Gulch was the general center of activity, little effort was made to build a town there as Benton, only 3.5 miles north, provided the services needed. Within the first decade almost $2 million was produced. In the next decade even more. Principal mines were: Cornucopia, Kerrick, Comanche, Eureka, Laura, Diana, and the Modoc.

In more recent years, the late 1940's on, mining activity in the Benton area has produced most of California's pumice. Although they had been known for many years, they were first worked in 1926. By 1948 eight firms were mining tens of thousands of tons each year by open-pit and underground methods. Its many uses include cleansing compounds, scouring agents, stucco, and accoustical plaster.

Further south in the Chidago, Wildrose, and Yellowjacket areas, more than three score mines have, over the years, added to Benton Station's importance as a general mining center.

Along the railroad line numerous towns began to grow. At Belleville several stamp mills and furnaces were built to serve the Candelaria mines in the hills. West of Montgomery Pass near Queen, the Indian Queen Mine produced ore enough to keep a 5-stamp mill and furnace busy.

Once the Carson & Colorado Railroad climbed what is now MONTGOMERY PASS through many twists, turns, tunnel, and trestles taking almost the same route as the present Highway 6 from Bishop to Tonopah. Although higher and steeper than the Donner Pass between San Francisco and Reno, with snowfall not nearly so heavy, this route is kept open all winter when Conway, Deadman, and Sherwin passes are all snowed in and impassable. Truck drivers can depend on it during the winter months.

GOLD FEVER COUNTRY
Tonapah - Goldfield

Almost two decades passed after the boom at Virginia City causing a steady decline in the economic strength of Nevada. Even the status of the state in national affairs was in question. With the discovery of gold at Tonopah in 1900 the downward trend was suddenly reversed. A new era was ushered in by more discoveries, boom towns, and vast sums of mineral wealth. Geographically speaking, most of the mining activity took place in the area just east of the California-Nevada border between Walker Lake and the Amargosa Desert. Economically, it set in motion many factors opening up the whole region between Carson City and Las Vegas. The latter grew from a few hundred to several thousand residents as it became a railhead to supply the mines and their attendant boom towns.

TONOPAH

Nevada has been referred to as "a land of geology by day and astronomy by night." It was to this setting in central Nevada that young Jim Butler came. A native of El Dorado County, California, he came well oriented in the life and ways of mining camps. Engaged in ranching he had seasonal opportunities to do some exploration of the Nevada hills.

In the spring of 1900 he set out to investigate two promising areas, one of them in the San Antonio Mountains which was reported by Indians to have possibilities.

While camping at some springs, called To-no-pah by the Indians, he made the discovery that was to change Nevada's history. The first assays in June showed possibilities of around $200 per ton. Not rich, but interesting. In typical rancher style he went home, finished his haying, put his affairs in order, and then returned in late August to the site he called Tonopah and staked his claim.

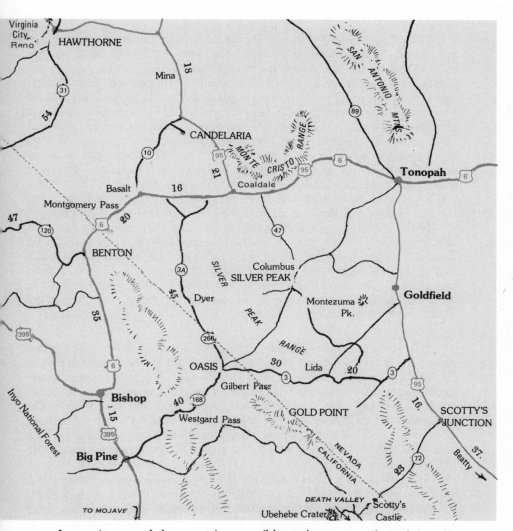

It was in one of the most inaccessible regions more than sixty miles from the nearest railroad station (Sodaville, on the Carson & Colorado Railroad). From the very beginning there were problems. Every gold miner experiences the same need for water, wood, and development money. Here was no exception. In a land where less than five inches of rain falls per year, there was no reserve to carry them through a long dry season. The local spring had to be supplemented with water packed by burros from nearby mountain springs. Native wood was adequate for cooking and heating but not suitable for timbering up the mines. Large sums of capital, so readily available in the Comstock days, was virtually non-existent now. Times were slow and mining stock was considered risky.

Undaunted, Butler borrowed a few dollars from a friend to get some supplies and then obtained the use of a wagon and teams by promising the owner a part interest in the "location" that would be made. First returns with pick, shovel, windlass and sweat produced two tons of ore that was shipped by freight team and railroad to Salt Lake City for reduction. He netted some $500 which was reinvested in needed equipment.

With development capital inaccessible a new concept in mining was introduced—leasing portions or "feet" of a claim. After costs were figured, the owner got one fourth and the miners got the rest. Scores of men got rich by this arrangement which soon spread to other camps where capital was short. The small working participant in the endeavor gave stability to mining that was absent from the operations where most of the capital was provided in speculative paper by investors living hundreds and thousands of miles away. In districts using the leasing system nearly all were verbal arrangements. It is interesting that few, if any, lawsuits were necessary to settle disagreements. In such camps as Virginia City the number of lawyers almost equalled the number of miners doing the digging. In most court settlements the prospector and developers would end up getting less out of the mines than did the lawyers who helped them save their interest.

With returns proven, a Philadelphia financier purchased the claim for almost a million dollars. Butler sold out and moved back to California. The Tonopah Mining Company was formed with capital in excess of one and a fourth million ending the practice there of leasing. A second mining company, the Tonopah Belmont was organized by Oddie, a former partner of Butler. These two companies accounted for more than half of all Tonopah's production over the years.

GOLDFIELD

Bill Marsh and Harry Stimler had either lucked out at Tonopah or they played a hunch card from the middle of the deck. Their prospecting at Rabbit Spring had produced little good—but it did give them some experience and a grubstake by Butler. They prospected the wild, open country between the Columbia Mountains and Malapae Mesa. On December 4, 1902 they located three claims about 25 miles south of Tonopah. It had been prospected many years before and passed over. This time Billy and Harry stayed with it and produced encouraging results over the next year.

Then in January, 1904 a rich strike at their claim changed everything for them. Soon thousands came, first from Tonopah, then from as far away as Reno and Las Vegas. Within months some 8000 people were prospecting and mining or engaged in business in Goldfield, as the new town was called. Leasers were taking out fabulous sums. One was reported as high as $10,000 in one day!

By 1905 more than a hundred mining companies and been organized. A post office and school had been opened. The town was surveyed to a plan and electricity had been introduced. It was brought across the mountains from Bishop over 100 miles away. Early in its development Goldfield had a population of over 20,000 and more than 200 buildings.

New bodies of rich ore were discovered in 1906 at the Hayes-Monetti mine. A new rush got under way when the word got out that returns were running as much as $30,000 in one day. The Tonopah and Tidewater and the Las Vegas and Tonopah railroads were hastily completed. Telephones and telegraph lines gave almost hourly reports with the San Francisco and eastern stock exchanges.

By 1907 several other mines developed in the neighboring area including Lida Junction, Gold Point, Gold Mountain and several short term towns. The "bust" to come was preceded by a boom as was seldom heard of from any camp. A single shipment from the Mohawk, amounting to less than 50 tons, brought over one half million dollars at a San Francisco smelter. By midsummer workers' and mine owners' differences, coupled with the nationwide financial panic, brought the operations temporarily to a hault. However, with the resumption of work in 1908 by the Goldfield Consolidated Mill production increased to a peak in 1910 of over $11 million. After 1911 the town lost most of its people. The last serious mining was done by the Consolidated Mining Company in 1919. By 1930 Goldfield had less than 1000 inhabitants—the fact that it was the county seat of Esmeralda County was about the only thing that saved it from becoming another member of the family of western ghost towns.

The first automobile arrived in Goldfield, August 10, 1904. A new era was born in the desert. With the arrival of motorized vehicles the days of the burro prospector and the long-line teams were numbered.

Roads were everywhere and anywhere and were little more than deepened wheel ruts in the sand and gravel. The 200 mile trip between Las Vegas and Goldfield was an experience. Extreme temperatures, scarcity of fuel and repair parts made the trips into the desert an adventure, hazardous at best. In some places toll roads were built and in others one made his own way when cloudbursts washed out sections of the regular built road. Soon county road districts were formed and regulations were passed to use them. In Tonopah the speed limit was 5 mph. Not to be outdone in progress, Goldfield set a speet limit of 6 mph, with vehicles drawn by horses having the right-of-way. But soon the hay-burners had to give way to the gas-guzzlers. Also in the mines, power equipment moved the earth and electricity processed the ores.

CANDELARIA—THE COLUMBUS MINING DISTRICT

The first claims were made by Mexican miners in 1864 and in the following year Candelaria, the claim, and the town came into being. By 69 the town had a population of some 900 with businesses, a post office and a school. The Columbus Mining District in Nevada also included the towns of Belleville and Columbus, which served the mining district. The community of Columbus, adjacent to Columbia Marsh supplied goods and services to the growing camps and became very active between 1872 to 1875. The town grew partly from the borax company operations at the Marsh, and in no small way, from the purchases made by the Candelaria miners. This included water packed in to them costing $1.50 a barrel and hauling their ore out at $8 a ton. The mining at Pickhandle Gulch expanded also. In an effort perhaps to defy such a dreary place, it changed its name from Pickhandle to Metalic City. Today, its name and a few old rock walls are about all that is left to remind us of those busy times.

Before railroads were extended into the area, heavy machinery, food and supplies were hauled by teams from lower Owens Valley. In summer the heat in the basins was simmering hot, in winter the sleet-laden winds in the pass through the Inyos and across the Fish Valley flatland were relentless. In early 1880 the Carson & Colorado Railroad was completed and began delivering supplies there.

To ease the water situation, a pipeline was constructed—mostly by Chinese and Mexican laborers. It extended from Trail Creek Canyon on the northeast slope of Boundary Peak to Candelaria. Through a series of diversions and troughs, the water emptied into a concrete reservoir. Then it was piped to the town as well as to the railroad. Not too long after all these improvements, Candelaria folded.

The Arrastra

The depressed rock-lined trough with the center stone post positioned the pole which was circled by a burro, mule or power source. The well-worn grooves were made by huge stones that were drug round and round in it crushing the ore.

SILVER PEAK

The story of Silver Peak is a classic example of working out great riches in low-grade ore. It could have been found by any wandering prospector audacious enough to venture into such a bleak place. The first discoveries were in 1863-64 when very few people were in this part of Nevada so little is known about the early days. No city with its attendant newspaper, or businesses, or houses were built there as many other accessible mining camps provided more attractive opportunities. It was first to last, a "company-town" operation. Also it could be mined only by equipment requiring large sums of money before returns became profitable.

On the north slope of Silver Peak were great quantities of silver and at Mineral Ridge just to the north was a field of gold ore. The big milling operations went through successive periods of large returns and suspended delays due to inadequate knowledge or equipment. At times they were losing more than they were taking out until new methods were developed. Interruptions were due to long periods of claims and counter-claims in lawsuits that dragged on for years trying to settle who really owned what. In 1871 Silver Peak was mostly deserted. Less than a half-dozen people were around. Then in 1878 new capital and enterprise had reopened the mines and huge returns were made. So it went over the decades. Overall, the Silver Peak mines showed a return of some $18 million.

The Foote Mineral Company had been producing lithium carbonate since 1966 just east of Silver Peak at the Clayton Valley Playa where there seems to be an unlimited supply of brine solutions.

As a contrasting footnote to this gigantic enterprise, at Silver Peak, the *American Journal of Mining,* issue of November, 1868 tells of a sturdy miner who worked his own small claim by employing an arrastra to break up his ore. Selecting the richest, he sacked it and hired Indians to pack it out over a tortuous trail in 100-pound bags to a mill. The use of the arrastra was employed by small operators all through the Basin Range country. The idea was first introduced by Mexican miners. Powered by hand, burros, or mules, or when available by waterwheel, the simple construction and operation made it readily adaptable to the reduction or ore rock to a pulverized mass that could then be "dry washed" or water panned.

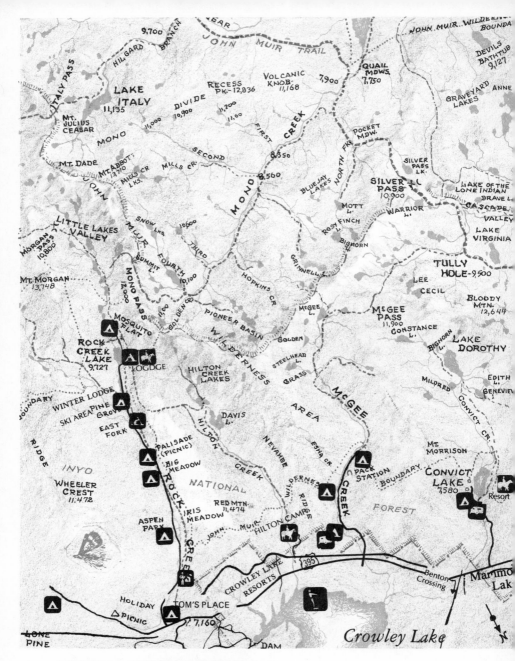

SIERRA-OWENS VALLEY

Backcountry trails lead to the lovely Hilton Creek lakes, upper Little Lakes Valley and just over Mono Pass to Pioneer Basin and the Mono Recesses. A strenuous trail leads to the headwaters of the East Fork to Tamarack Lakes and over Morgan Pass to the head waters of Pine Creek. Full services are available at Tom's Place with stores and more than a dozen campgrounds in the area.

152

Bloody Mountain, Lake Dorothy

ROCK CREEK-McGEE CREEK
CONVICT LAKE-CROWLEY LAKE

For years this area has provided continuous good fishing for thousands of visitors. Natural reproduction and scheduled stocking by the Fish & Game has maintained a consistent number of fish for anglers of all ages. Repeated visits over the past few seasons indicate an unusual take by pre-teen age kids as well as general satisfaction by the old time Issac Waltoners.

The various waters enable a variety of angling experiences:

Rock Creek and the backcountry of Little Lakes Valley.

Crowley Lake and the Owens River between it and Bishop.

The lakes of upper Hilton Creek Basin.

McGee Creek and its headwater lakes.

Convict Lake and the large lakes at the head of Convict Creek.

Rock Creek and Little Lakes Valley lie along a north-south course in a deep glacial trough between Wheeler Ridge and the main Sierra Front. The streams of the six-mile long Little Lakes Valley rise below active glaciers near Mt. Dodd and Mt. Abbott. Its many pocket meadows are a glory of sub-alpine wildflowers in early summer. The numerous 13,000' plus peaks along their Sierra backdrop are a delight to photographers.

McGEE CREEK

There are three Forest Service campgrounds in the short distance between Hwy. 395 and the boundary of the John Muir Wilderness. Above there permits are required for day or overnight use. The headwaters rise in more than a half dozen lakes along the northeast wall of Glacier Divide. The McGee Pass Trail leads to the Tully Hole junction of the John Muir-Pacific Crest Trail and the Cascade Valley fishing country. Most often taken are rainbows and Eastern brooks, although several higher lakes contain goldens.

153

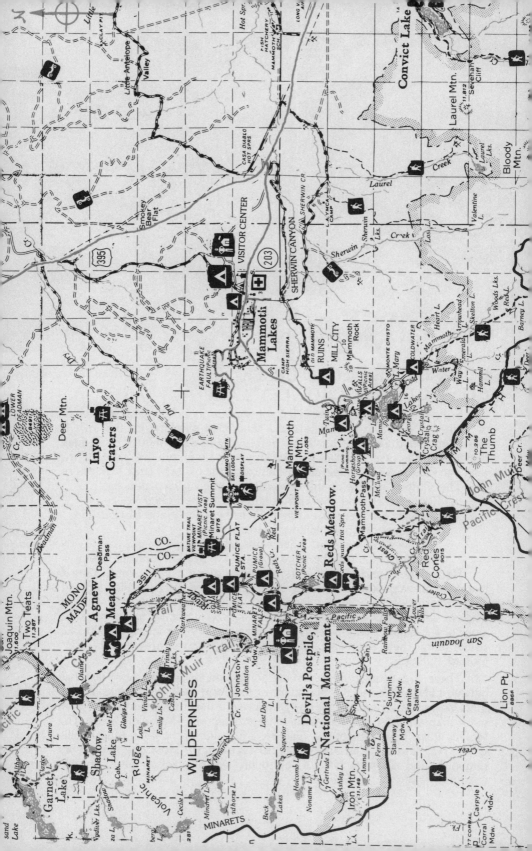

MAMMOTH LAKES

The first thing to do when entering this vacation area is to stop in at the Visitor Center of the Forest Service which offers exhibits about the country, maps, permits, information on their programs, local events, and backcountry trip planning. Their programs include short walks in the Mammoth area, auto tours, illustrated talks and in the winter appropriate snow activities.

ONE DAY CAR TRIPS

Earthquake Fault: A self-guiding tour in and around the fifty-foot earth split.

Minaret Vista: At the summit of the ridge overlooking the San Joaquin Valley.

Devils Postpile - Reds Meadow - Sotcher Lake

Lookout Mountain Viewpoint

Obsidian Dome and Inyo Craters

Hot Springs State Fish Hatchery—where 20 million trout eggs are produced per year and some 4 million fingerlings and 600,000 catchable trout are planted in lakes and streams.

Old Mammoth and the Mammoth Mill site

Mammoth Mountain Ski Lift Area

Sherwin Creek Canyon—especially in the spring when wildflowers are at their best

A tour around the Mammoth Lakes

SHORT AND ONE DAY HIKING TRIPS

Mammoth Mountain from Twin Lakes

Sherwin Creek Lakes

The Postpile from the Ranger Station

Agnew Meadows to Shadow Lake or Rosalie Lake

Rainbow Falls from Reds Meadow or Devils Postpile

155

MAMMOTH HISTORY

The glint of sunlight on bits of yellow gold or blue-gray silver taken from eastern Sierra mines were never to match the rewards of its snowy peaks, sky-blue lakes and deep green forests. And so it has been with Mammoth Lakes. By the late 1800's "gold fever" had become an incurable malady infecting the poorest one-pair-of-pants prospector and the wealthiest railroad builder. No place was safe from their inspection between Death Valley flats to Sierra meadows. Then, when the best guesses had been checked out, came the day of the great gambles—the search for "lost" mines. Tales of the '49ers, of half-crazy prospectors suffering from desert heat, and "investment promoters", passed on the stories of such lost mines as the Lost Gunsight and the Lost Breyfogle mines in the Death Valley country. The eastern Sierra, too, was to have its "lost" mine—the *Lost Cement Mine* where gold nuggets resembled large "raisins in a pudding". The desire-to-believe led the prospectors into the Mammoth region. No Lost Cement Mine was found but they did find gold and silver that started a new rush in June, 1877.

Within a year more than 1500 people had been attracted to Mammoth City. New roads were built between the strike and Bodie and Bishop. A toll-trail was built between Oakhurst (then called Fresno Flats) to bring in supplies from the San Joaquin Valley. Part of this route is now known as the French or Old Mammoth Trail extending between Clover Meadows and Mammoth.

The new camp developed rapidly. Much of the production was from the Mammoth Mine which yielded $200,000 in 1878-81. By 1887 a mining district was formed. Several thousand people lived in the make-shift "cities" of Mammoth City, Mill City and Pine City. But the returns soon began to fade. Some mining was done in the late 1890's and early 1900's and 1930's. More activity took place from 1954-58. Production has been more than $1.5 million total. Principal mines were: Argosy, Beauregard—$1,000,000, Don Quixote, Lisbon, Mammoth—$200,000, Mammoth Consolidated—$100,000, Monte Cristo—$100,000, and the Sierra Group. Total actually developed costs on these mines exceeded their total return.

Today's visitors find little evidence of the old mining days except the remains of a few log cabins, pieces of machinery here and there and great piles of rock near diggings resembling abandoned coyote holes.

Bunk House & Mill at Mammoth

Courtesy of Inyo National Forest

Some thirty years drifted by with only intermittent explorations for pay-dirt. Ranching in the Owens Valley became more stabilized. During the summers, Valley people and their visitors began camping out in the Mammoth area. Between 1920 and 1930 tent cabins were built at Lake Mary, Lake Mamie, and Twin Lakes to accommodate paying guests. Like the Curry's camp in Yosemite, the ventures here soon caught on with visitors from the "outside". Fishing, hunting and family camping soon became the major industry of what was to be known as Sierra East.

By 1938 the new township of Mammoth was established. Two years later a winter sports group initiated ski races and Dave McCoy set up the first rope-tow on Mammoth Mountain. In a few years permanent buildings were erected to house year round activities. Campgrounds were completed by the Forest Service at several locations. The green gold of the forests and white gold of nearby snowy peaks assured the success of Mammoth as a recreation area.

Mill City Kelsey Sierra Studio

Minarets—Backcountry in Winter

Rocky Rockwell

MAMMOTH BACKCOUNTRY TRIPS

Mammoth Pass: Trailhead near Horseshoe Lake (8960'). Trail leads west past McLeod Lake about one mile to Mammoth Pass (9300'). From there trails lead to Reds Meadow and the Devils Postpile. It junctions with the John Muir-Pacific Crest Trail near the Red Cone.

Mammoth Crest: Trailhead near Lake George (9008'). Climbs 1500 feet in two miles to the crest. From there it follows southeast along the crest for three miles to an elevation above 11,000'. Vast panoramic views of the upper Owens Valley and the Basin Range country to the east. Also, to the west down the broad forested basins of the San Joaquin. Good loop could include Duck Lake and return via the Duck Pass-Coldwater Canyon Trail to Lake Mary.

Minarets Wilderness (Hiking and Horseback). Trails from Reds Meadow or Agnew Meadows trailheads leading to the many lakes adjacent to the Minaret Crest, Thousand Island Lake, Shadow Lake, and Garnet Lake. All are spectacular in their beauty with the mighty Banner and Ritter in the background.

For more detailed information, see JOHN MUIR TRAIL COUNTRY by Lew & Ginny Clark with 4-color maps and photographs.

158

June and Gull Lakes   Courtesy of Inyo National Forest

JUNE LAKE LOOP

The streams and lakes in Reversed Creek Canyon have provided anglers and family campers with many hours of enjoyment in fishing with pleasant mountain campsites for many years. Now in winter it is a mecca for winter sports with ski and tows and lifts. Originally it was called Horseshoe Canyon by the surveyor for the government, due to the lakes and streams at the base of the mountain formation.

Visitors have been puzzled by the unusual fact that the largest lake and stream flows west toward the Sierra instead of away from them. As geologists explain it, the Rush Creek glacier and other tributary ice flows from Koip Peak crest cut deeper into the valley northward along the Rush Creek course to Mono Lake than was possible through the much harder bedrock of Oh! Ridge. It was a large glacier covering the entire Rush Creek basin westward to the Mt. Dana Koip Peak's eastward slope. Several small glaciers are still found along the shaded north side of the Ritter Range and at Koip Peak.

Approaching June Lake from Oh! Ridge the visitor is aware of a huge boulder perched by the road on top of other huge rocks. It is larger than a double garage with an estimated weight of almost a thousand tons. This is an erratic. Picked up along the way by a glacier from a distant canyon wall, it was dragged to here and left when the glacier melted. The southern rim of the glacier flow is marked by the ridge between Mt. Dana and the San Joaquin Mountain which includes Island and Agnew passes.

The beauty of June Lake is not seasonal. Each time of the year special mountain landscapes inspire visitors—spring wildflowers and full-bodied creeks bubbling with snowy run-offs; lazy summer breeze with aspens quivering; the brilliant yellow, gold, and orange leaves mixed with the dark green evergreens against the gray granite hillsides of autumn, and the chilling beauty of a snow fall covering the mighty peaks.

JUNE LAKE HISTORY

That Indians found Reversed Creek Canyon and its lakes good hunting has been apparent by the remains of old campsites. The Jeffrey pine forest to the east and its attendant game provided shelter, fuel, and food in winter. In summer they moved into the higher mountain areas where pinyon nuts supplemented their diet. Long before the arrival of white settlers and prospectors, a regular trade route had been in use between the Mono Paiutes and the Miwoks of Yosemite. While working as backcountry patrol ranger in Yosemite, I found numerous evidences of "rancheria" type meeting places near Mono Pass and Donohue Pass. At a tarn near McClure glacier was more than a bushel basket of scattered obsidian chips and faulted arrow points obviously discarded and left in this meeting place where the obsidian from the Owens Valley area was traded for acorns from Yosemite. Later, Mono Pass became a principal west-east pack route across the Sierra for the first prospectors and miners interested in the Mono Lake country.

Good fishing in the deep lakes led to building of Carson's Camp in 1921—the first of many to follow in Horseshoe Canyon. With the building of the dam for the water and power at the lower end of the marshy valley, Grant Valley was born. It holds the overflow waters of Rush, Parker, Lee Vining and Walker creeks before going into Owens River and Crowley Lake. The lakes of the Loop are now well stocked by the Fish and Game Department to provide good catches.

Winter has been a mixed blessing and disaster for the June Lake people. During the long winters snow piles to great depths and over the years avalanches have taken their toll. In 1915 the first ski tows came to the valley and the following year electricity was brought into the area to run the rope-tow and light their homes. Then in 1960 the U.S. Forest Service granted a lease to build the June Mountain Ski Lift. Expansion since then has provided additional ski facilities and turned it into a great winter sports center.

MONO BASIN COUNTRY

The Mono Basin presents a startling contrast between the towering east front of the Sierra and the Basin Ranges. The Sierra front rises more than 6000′ above the arid basin surrounding Mono Lake. Its face is broken into deep, glacial scarred canyons separated by narrow, ragged, ridges. Its general environment includes Mono Lake and its neighboring plain, extensive volcanic craters, flows, and domes, and, some half dozen glacier formed canyons.

To the east of Hwy. 395 the landscape presents an unreal group of phantom like hills—the Mono Craters. They extend from the south side of Mono Lake some ten miles southward. They consist of a group of pumice cones in which domes of obsidian (volcanic glass) have risen. The group makes up the Mono Range. In several cases the craters were filled to overflowing onto the adjacent plain. The most northern dome near the lake is called Panum Crater—just a short distance from Hwy. 120. Beyond there, some five or six miles, several roads lead south along the eastern front of the Mono Crater Range. Return west to junction with Hwy. 395 can be made by the interesting Devils Punchbowl just east of June Lake or via the Aeolian Buttes. The Devils Punchbowl is a small but well preserved explosion cone. Its crater is some 1200′ in diameter and 140 feet deep. In the bottom is a small obsidian plug 40 feet high and 250 feet in diameter.

Rocky Rockwell

INYO CRATERS

These craters have the distinction of being young geologically—less than 2000 years old, and containing water. These explosive craters indicate the volcanic action in this area. The Obsidian Dome, Mono Craters, Casa Diablo Hot Springs and the numerous other hot springs in Long Valley area exemplify the tremendous forces that once took place. The pumice rocks and white soil cover the country for miles around to a great depth.

162

Mono Craters   Rocky Rockwell

MONO LAKE

Mono Lake lies in a fault basin surrounded by volcanic debris. Its water is somewhat saltier than the ocean and contains little life except for a heavy brine-tolerant fly and shrimp. The lake, about 10 x 14 miles across, has had a depth of more than the present 150'. Old wave markings indicate a shoreline when it was almost a thousand feet deep. The recent years of drought and evaporation, plus the diversion of the Rush Creek to the Los Angeles Aqueduct, have reduced the waters to a point where it seems probable that it will be dry in the not too distant future.

The fresh waters of the ancient lake came from melting glaciers of the eastern Sierra between Rush Creek basin and the Conway Summit area. These glaciers moved wastward down from the rising Sierra block building lateral moraines up to 800 feet high as they went. These are quite evident at the exits of Bloody, Gibs, and Lee Vining canyons.

There are two islands in the lake which invite exploration. These were formed by volcanic eruptions in the old lakebed area that were an extension of the same activity that created the Mono Craters. Seeing large flocks of sea gulls so far from the ocean is a surprising sight. Actually, the area attracts them annually in the spring to nest and rear their young, in the fall returning to the coast. The largest islands, Paoha, has cold and hot flowing springs and a small lake in its volcanic formed crater. There are also descendants of numerous rabbits and goats that were left there by early settlers. The smaller island, Negit, is host to the largest sea gull rookery in the west.

163

The tufa towers of Mono Lake are subject to much speculation as to their exact origins. In general, they were built up in the waters of the lake when it was much deeper. They were made up of the accumulation of plant life around upflowing calcareous waters from fresh water springs out of the bottom of the lake. Exposed to air they have solidified into their present interesting forms that invite photography during the late afternoon when shadows accentuate their contours.

Rocky Rockwell

The region has produced few indications of mining over the years. However, at Mono Mills a sawmill was built that drew upon the extensive Jeffrey pines forest nearby. Wood and lumber in large quantities was needed at Bodie just north of the lake. Eventually, a narrow gauge railway was built to haul lumber to the mines to keep up with its needs.

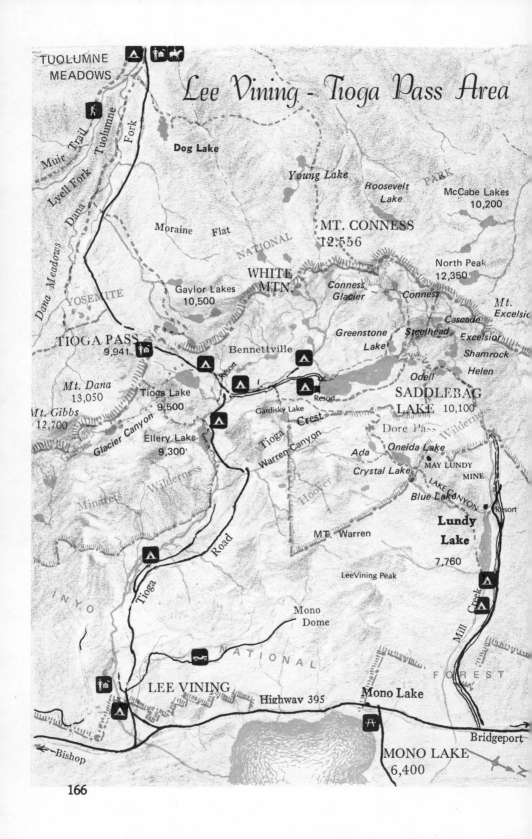

Lee Vining - Tioga Pass Area

TUOLUMNE
MEADOWS

Muir Trail

Lyell Fork

Dana

Tuolumne Fork

Dana Meadows

YOSEMITE

Dog Lake

Moraine Flat

Young Lake

Roosevelt Lake

MT. CONNESS
12,556

McCabe Lakes
10,200

NATIONAL

WHITE MTN.

North Peak
12,350

PARK

Gaylor Lakes
10,500

Conness Glacier

Conness

Mt. Excelsior

TIOGA PASS
9,941

Bennettville

Greenstone Lake

Cascade

Steelhead

Excelsior

Shamrock

Resort

Helen

Mt. Dana
13,050

Tioga Lake
9,500

Gardisky Lake

Resort

Odell

SADDLEBAG
LAKE   10,100

Mt. Gibbs
12,700

Glacier Canyon

Ellery Lake
9,300'

Crest

Warren Canyon

Dore Pass

Wilderness

Ada

Oneida Lake

Crystal Lake

MAY LUNDY
MINE

Minarets

Wilderness

Tioga

Hoover

MT. Warren

Blue Lake

LAKE CANYON

Resort

Lundy
Lake

7,760

Tioga

Road

I N Y O

LeeVining Peak

Mono
Dome

NATIONAL

Mill Creek

F O R E S T

LEE VINING

Highway 395

Mono Lake

Bridgeport

Bishop

Mono Lake

MONO LAKE
6,400

Tioga Pass, Down Canyon   Kelsey Sierra Studio

LEE VINING-LUNDY

North-south bound travelers on Hwy. 395 are usually so engaged with the expansive view across Mono Lake Basin they pass unaware of Lundy or Lee Vining canyons. Closed most of the year by deep snow and ice, it has been passed by except in summer when they use it as a passageway over Tioga Pass to Yosemite. However, fisherman and campers wanting an uncrowded area come back here year after year. Complete information about it can be had at the Ranger Station just west of Lee Vining. The region includes excellent camp sites and stream or lake fishing. Unusually large fish have been taken from Saddlebag.

The abrupt east front of the Sierra is a climaxing contrast to the sage flats surrounding Mono Lake. Glaciers lie along the shaded north faces of Mt. Dana (13,050') and Mt. Conness (12,556'). Below Ellery Lake the stream follows down the deep, glacial groved canyon. Above Ellery a high glacial basin extends north parallel to the crest. Of the more than a dozen lakes there, Saddlebag is the largest. Eleven small lakes at the headwaters of Mine Creek also provide good fishing. Trails (or a boat taxi) lead to the head of Saddlebag Lake basin. The Greenstone-Conness lakes above consistently provide good fishing. From there it is an easy day trip to the foot of Conness Glacier or, by keeping to the south of it, follow the route to the top of Mt. Conness. A limited, walk-in campground is at the site of an old sawmill. The entire upper basin presents a sublime, low-key mountain experience quite removed from the extravagant traffic on the Tioga-Tuolumne Meadows road.

BENNETTVILLE

Even this remote, sub-alpine country did not escape the persistent efforts of the gold seekers. Today's visitor will find a few reminders of yesterday's dreams about a mile from the Tioga Lodge at the ghost town of Bennettville. The most permanent thing done was the building of the Great Sierra Wagon Road (now Hwy. 120 over the Tioga Pass), an empty tunnel driven 1,784 feet into the mountain, a few pieces of machinery and, propped up here and there by great rocks, a few weather-scarred poles that carried the Great Sierra telephone Line between Lundy and Bennettville, head-quarters of the Great Sierra Consolidated Mining Company at the end of the Great Sierra Wagon Road! What a day for dreamers trying to make it big out of a shepherd boy's claim!

The gold-bearing outcrops were discovered in 1860 but repeated prospecting efforts over the next twenty years revealed little to reward their investment of more than $300,000. In the rush some 350 claims were located near the surface quartz veins and the mineralized metamorphic rocks. Tioga Mine received the most attention where its developers were convinced they could hit the main lode by driving horizontally on the hillside with a tunnel. Hope was high. Perhaps another Comstock or Bodie was here. The road was built from Groveland, one hundred miles west in the Sierra foothills, to the mine. Dana City and Bennettville housed them in this bleak mountain canyon, while the Great Sierra Consolidated Silver Company was driving the Great Sierra Tunnel. The company failed in 1884. Later extensions in 1933-34 encountered nothing of value.

168

Lundy Camp

Courtesy of Inyo National Forest

The Lundy Trail from the Tioga Campground area crosses Tioga Crest and down Lake Canyon to Lundy Lake. This is the route of the old Miner's Trail that ran between the Tioga Mine and Lundy and extended on east to Bodie. About 1.5 miles up on this route a trail branches to Gardinsky Lake, a very scenic area lying just north of Tioga Peak (11,532'). A cross-country trip from there leads into the almost unexplored backcountry of upper Warren Canyon basin.

Glacier Canyon Creek rises at the foot of Dana Glacier. Conducted trips to the glacier, the summit of Mt. Dana or the interesting Dana Plateau are usually made each summer by Ranger Naturalists at Tuolumne Meadows. Inquire there for information about routes. The mountain here presents a striking contrast of Sierra granites of the Conness Crest and the metamorphic reds and yellows of rock in the Dana Plateau-Mt. Warren group.

Lundy Canyon was also carved out by branches of the ancient Conness Glacier field. Evidences of such activity are seen at its lower lateral moraines and on up Mill Creek to the many ponds found at its headwaters near North Peak. Other than a store, a few cabins, and scattered camping spots little has been developed.

The building of a sawmill in the canyon in 1878 to cut lumber for Bodie led, the following year, to the discovery of gold in upper Lake Canyon. the town of Wasson grew up near the May Lundy Mine and a toll road was built to supply the camp. The area had been prospected during the Comstock silver rush of the 1860's but the Lundy Lode was not discovered until 1877. The mine was worked on a major scale until 1911 and reworked in the late 1930's. Total production was in excess of $3 million.

Matterhorn Crest   Russ Johnson

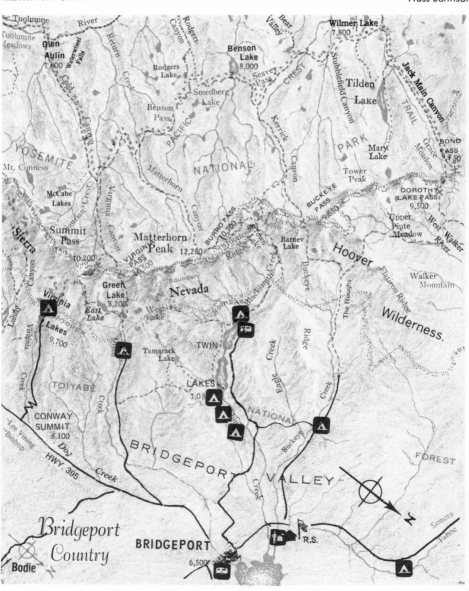

BRIDGEPORT VALLEY

"Big Meadows" was the name of the country in early days, and with good reason. Its many square miles of open meadow are bounded on the north by the Sweetwater Mountains, the east by the Bodie Hills, to the west rises the Sierra in a culmination of broken crests at Sawtooth Ridge and Matterhorn Peak (12,264').

It is a setting that breathes a feeling of reality into the legends of Fremont, Kit Carson, and pioneers who passed through here. Ghost towns of early mining camps are still evident in such places as China Camp, Aurora, and Bodie. Other places have become only names on the maps.

Bridgeport has outlasted its passing parade of scouts, wagon trains, and miners due to its extensive stock raising and the kind of people who love the place. The old courthouse, built in 1880, was constructed of handmade bricks hauled in from Bodie. It is one of the oldest courthouses in America that is still in use. A museum of early Bridgeport days is located nearby in what formerly was the schoolhouse. A visit to these places might well precede an extended trip through the diggings of the Bodie Hills.

DOGTOWN-MONOVILLE (1857-1860, 1880)

The high country just north of Mono Lake separates the deserty Mono Valley from the Big Meadows (Bridgeport) basin. Beyond Conway Summit streams flow northeast into the East Walker River country. First gold mining ventures in this region began before the Civil War a little south of Bridgeport on Dog Creek. Placer washing in 1857 produced enough gold to start another rush—where there was *placer* gold, surely there would be a lode in the hills! Some Mormon boys from Nevada soon moved in and extended the operations. Within two years Dogtown was a busy place. When more evidences were found in the southern hills just east of Conway Summit, claims were staked in every gulch and along any promising ridge. There, Monoville was born, the first real gold rush diggings east of the Sierra.

Gold mining and gold miners need water to operate. Everyone threw in together to build a ditch to bring in water from Virginia Creek. However, returns were scattered. Between the freezing cold of winter and the discovery of rich silver deposits in Aurora the migratory flock of prospectors took off again for better pickings. In later years, around 1880, the old Mono Diggings were reworked by hydraulic tools and took almost $100,000 out of the Sinnamon Cut at the head of Bacon Gulch.

SWEETWATER MOUNTAINS-SWEETWATER DIGGINGS

Between the crest of the Sweetwater Mountains and Sweetwater creek in Nevada, numerous small streams encouraged some prospecting in the early 1860's. The principal period of activity came later between 1880 and 1884, when more than $500,000 was produced. Accurate data on such type of individual placer mining is unlikely to reflect the real returns. The principal mines were: Kentuck, Frederick, Silverado, Star & Great Western, and Longstreet. Early settlements were at Belfort, Monte Cristo, and Star City.

MASONIC: This area northeast of Bridgeport was prospected for some years before and after the Comstock rush of 1860. Valuable ore was not discovered until 1902. The chief period of production was 1907-1910. The Cheming Mine has been worked intermittently in recent years. Principal mines were the Serita, $500,000; Pittsburg-Liberty, $700,000; and the Chemung, $60,000.

AURORA—"GODDESS OF THE DAWN"

Evidences of gold and silver were found in 1860 by a prospecting party bound for Mono Lake. The following rush brought in miners from Monoville. Within a few months the town was laid out and named Aurora— Goddess of the Dawn. It grew rapidly and in a year there were 2000 citizens. Then returns began to dwindle and talk of other places lured men away.

The attractions of Aurora were sought by the citizens of two counties and two states. The old von Schmidt survey had set the Nevada-California boundary showing Aurora "just inside California". For a time it was considered accordingly and Aurora was declared the county seat of Mono County. The following fall Nevada declared Aurora the seat of Nevada's Esmeralda County. This situation lasted for nearly two years. To settle the matter the legislatures of the two states sponsored a joint survey. While it was being made election time arrived. Citizens voted for a full set of Mono County officials at the police station. Then, they went across the street to the Armory Hall and voted for a set of county officials for Esmeralda County, Nevada. In three weeks the survey crew set the state boundary four miles *west* of Aurora. By wagon the records and equipment of the Mono County government was moved to Bodie; later it was moved west to Big Meadows, later to be called Bridgeport.

OTHER GOLD GHOST TOWNS OF NEVADA

CHINESE CAMP: These historical sites lie just east of the Nevada State line halfway between Aurora and Masonic. Although several mines were developed in this region production was limited to a few just north of Sugarloaf Peak. Nevada historical maps show China Camp, Chinese Camp, and Homestead Mine as centers of the most activity, most of which was in placer mining and little was left when they were worked out.

In almost every mining camp there was a Chinatown. They built the railroads and pipelines, cut wood, carried rocks and ores on their backs, and some mined their own claims. They worked in laundries, mills, and restaurants. They had their own customs, stores, and settlements. When they moved, they went on foot packing their few belongings into baskets suspended on a long pole they balanced on their neck by a handmade yoke. They were an industrious, polite people who gave friendship and kindness in return for friendship and kindness and kept pretty well to themselves.

Aurora   Rocky Rockwell

BODIE

Not many mining camps were named after their discoverers. Most of them appear related to lost burros, King Soloman, Yellow Dog, Last Chance, Rusty Pick, etc. Occasionally the crusty shell of a lonely prospector developed a crack in it and a little sentiment was exposed as he christened his treasure after Lucy Jo, Henrietta, Mary Anna or even after the popular singer of those days, Jenny Lind. (The more remote the diggings the more often the ladies' names were used!) The big mines at Bodie bore the names of their syndicate or consolidation—no ladies.

It was some eight or nine years after the '49er Rush. Prospectors were searching every lead on the hills east of the Sierra. Traces were found near Mono Lake at Dogtown and Monoville. The Comstock discovery at Virginia City brought thousands back over the hills. In '59 William Bodie and a few companions were prospecting north of Mono Lake. In July they found evidences of placer gold and built a cabin to house them while they explored their prospects. It proved to be a rough winter. When they finally headed out for Monoville, Bodie became ill. He became too weak to walk and died in the snowstorm. Covering him with loose stones, his partners pushed on back to the mine. When the snow melted his body was found and buried where it had lain all winter. It was not until the summer of 1871 that the winter grave was found again and William Bodie's remains were brought back to the site where he had found gold.

In the spring following Bodie's death, claims were stacked and a district organized. But activity was minor until 1872 when rich ore was found and the rush was on with much production from rich but shallow deposits. The town was scattered on a flat about one-half mile wide by two miles long. In 1878 it had less than two hundred homes, an active business district, and a population of 1500. Half of them were out of work. Of the 700 "locations", less than a half dozen were sound with only the Bodie, the Standard Mine, and the Bulwar the most profitable.

By 1879 as production increased in the big mines, Bodie grew to more than 5000. Fifteen to twenty freight teams were required to haul in the necessary supplies. Several daily stages ran to Aurora and Bridgeport. With two dozen saloons, and almost as many lawyers, it attracted all those who had long, cold winters, and its many men idle most of the time led to lawless conditions which merited the expression "The Bad Men of Bodie". Those who had missed it now in Bodie were out to prove that if they couldn't make it big, they could at least be the badest! Stage robberies and killings became almost a daily occurrence.

175

It took unbelievable quantities of wood to keep the mines operating and the town warm. With the cold weather and hard times for many, people began drifting to other camps. Even the hardy Chinese began leaving. Wood was scarce and more was needed than could be cut from the hills to the west and hauled in by teams. A narrow-gauge railroad was built between Bodie and Mono Mills, south of Mono Lake in the Jeffrey pine forest.

The peak production was in 1881 when ten to twelve thousand people lived in the town. In 1893 it became one of the first mining camps to use electricity. After 1912 there was reduced activity, many mines folded, and the railroad was abandoned. A severe fire destroyed a good part of the town in 1932. The Bureau of Mines reports show that Bodie was the most productive district in the Basin Range country producing more than $30 million. It had also yielded over one million ounces of silver!

All photographs on this page by Ernest Hommerding

All photographs on this page by Ernest Hommerding

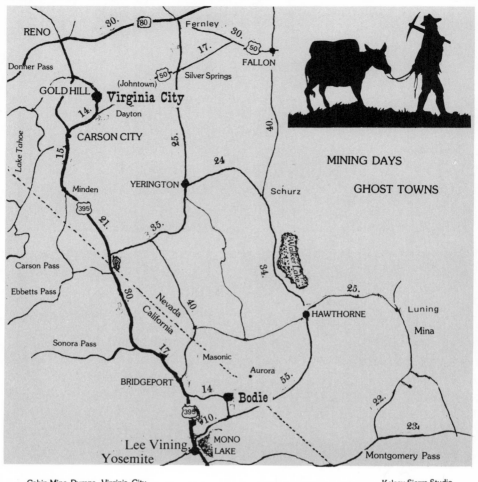

RENO
Donner Pass
80
30.
Fernley
30.
17.
FALLON
50
50
Silver Springs
GOLD HILL
(Johntown)
Virginia City
Dayton
14.
CARSON CITY
Lake Tahoe
15.
Minden
25.
24.
395
21.
85.
Schurz
YERINGTON
Carson Pass
30.
40.
Walker Lake
34.
Ebbetts Pass
Nevada
California
25.
HAWTHORNE
Luning
Sonora Pass
17.
Masonic
Aurora
55.
Mina
BRIDGEPORT
14.
Bodie
22.
395
10.
23.
Lee Vining
MONO LAKE
Yosemite
Montgomery Pass

MINING DAYS

GHOST TOWNS

Cabin-Mine Dumps, Virginia City

Kelsey Sierra Studio

VIRGINIA CITY IN 1878

THE COMSTOCK LODE: The First Hooraw!

The discovery of the famous Comstock Lode initiated a series of mining activity that attracted enough people into the Nevada Territory to help it to become a state, as well as supplying more than one-quarter billion dollars into the Federal Treasury.

By 1855 the chances of striking it rich in the California goldfields began to fade. The best places were all taken or washed out. The expensive process of sinking deep shafts and financing huge mining operations froze out the small prospector. They began to reconsider their hasty trek to California and recalled interesting looking rocks they had seen on their way out. After a decade of declining returns a happy incident sparked what was to become the west's wildest mining venture—the Comstock. Many who had sailed around the Horn to get to the goldfields were now walking across the Sierra to seek the treasures of the Basin Ranges. Over the next thirty years the area produced almost $300 million in gold and silver to change the course of Nevada and California history.

In the sagebrush-covered hills east of Lake Tahoe was a small shanty town called Johntown with a dozen makeshift shelter-buildings and a collection of tired, hungry, dispirited men. The placer mining was dwindling and the men were disgusted with the blue-stuff they had to put up with in their search for gold. Two brothers, Allen and Hosea Grosh were the first to recognize the possible value of the blue-stuff and Allen made some tests and took notes on these findings. Hosea died in a mining accident and Allen, trying to get to California where he could further prove out his analysis of the silver potential, died in the freezing winter crossing of the Sierra.

179

Masonic Cemetery, Virginia City   Kelsey Sierra Studio

This was the setting of the drama that was to be produced with a cast of characters such as "Old Pancake" Comstock, the usual camp hanger-on, and a couple of hard working, determined Irishmen who scoured the hills for miles around, and, to be added to the cast George Hearst, Flood, and Ralston. All later became great names in San Francisco. Two Irishmen, Peter O'Riley and Patrick McLaughlin were prospecting in Six-Mile Canyon. While testing some likely looking dirt near "old man Caldwell's Spring" they found unusual black dirt. Gold Canyon had been pretty well worked out by placer miners, so they had moved up to a low summit called Gold Hill. Their first test showed good color in the pan!

Their feverish efforts produced more and they had panned some $300 in dust when one of the Johnstown camp drifters, Old Pancake stopped by. He was, by far, the laziest man in the diggings. They called him Old Pancake because he was too lazy to make bread. But he was not one to overlook an opportunity for easy pickings. He soon bluffed his way into a partnership with O'Riley and McLaughlin claiming he owned the spring they were using.

The blue-stuff found was almost pure silver and gold, when assayed at Nevada City, was worth $3,000 a ton! The news spread. A flood of hungry prospectors left the California fields and headed east. Two camps, Gold Hill and Virginia City, soon bulged with miners. Old Pancake's loose tongue advertised *his* mine so much men began referring to the discovery as "... old Comstock's mine".

The rush to Washoe was on. For most of them they got their fill of excitement being in the wildest town of the west. But they were placer mine men. The riches here were encased in a great fault line zone. The lode had been developed when heated fluids bearing minerals had flowed into a massive fissure caused by massive subterranean faulting where both silver and gold were deposited in great quantities.

180

As thousands poured in from all over Nevada and California, Virginia City erupted into a bawdy city. More than $15 million was taken out in the next four years. The operation followed the customary pattern—big stakes took big equipment and vast sums of capital to develop them. The little fellows couldn't handle that kind of mining. Soon the glory-hole seekers moved on to find their own "Comstock" in the mountains of the Basin Ranges. For a while they were scattered to the areas west of Walker Lake where Esmeralda strike was made, and to the Humboldt Mountains northeast of Washoe.

Excitement at Virginia City faded for a time. Then in 1873 four mines formed the Consolidated Virginia to test their belief that the comstock Lode grew wider and deeper into the Davidson Mountain. Staking their work, and all the capital they could raise, they drove a shaft down into the tough rock more than 1000 feet. There they found a lode that was over fifty feet wide filled with gold and silver. Mark Twain was there to capture the color and the excitement of the times. His tales in "Roughing It" are a classic description of Gold Fever activity.

It was not evenly distributed in the lode. When a large deposit was found it was called a "bonanza" (in Spanish, "clear skies"); those getting only barren rocks were in a "borrasca" (storm). The Comstock Lode, two and a half miles long, lay between Gold Hill and Six-Mile Canyon—the Ophir Mine at one end, the Gold Hill placer diggings at the other.

Catholic Church, Virginia City

Some 17,000 claims were "located". An explosion of speculation activities followed. Most of them worthless. More than half of the total product of the Comstock and all the dividends came out of the two pairs of adjacent mines. The Crown Point and Belcher, and, the Consolidated and California.

The venture has been referred to as a "suburb" of San Francisco. It had been San Francisco's capital that paid for the great quantities of mining equipment needed to work this kind of mine. It was San Franciscans who received most of its return. Over trails and dirt roads it was hauled out of the sage flats near Virginia City to the bank vaults in the City of the Golden Gate.

The Hearst fortune began here in 1850 when George Hearst, who had been haunted by only "indifferent success at Nevada City and Grass Valley" was about to pull out. He was an industrious, hard worker who had slaved for years to make it. By 1859 he had had about enough. Then he heard "in confidence" about the assay of ore from a new discovery to the east of Mt. Davidson. On foot, he hurried over the mountains. Though all the area had been "located", their owners were without funds to develop them. They were eager to get hold of some capital and sold Hearst one-sixth interest in the Ophir. Back over the mountains he went. Selling a mine he owned at Nevada City and borrowing $1000 from a hotel keeper friend, he then returned east to the Washoe to conclude his buy-in on the Ophir. It was to become the richest mine in history. Two arrastras were built and some thirty-odd tons of selected ore was sacked. Mules packed it across the Sierra trail to Sacramento, then on to San Francisco by boat for smelting. This first mule train load of devilish blue-stuff, paid Hearst and the co-owners, above the cost of transportation and smelting, $9100 ... and it was only the beginning!

Fifty-seven percent of the mine was silver and forty-three percent was gold. To process the ore a stamp mill was packed in by mules from California, although some of the highest grade ore was sent to England for smeltering.

By 1860 they had ten more men working at the mine. At first Mexican miners were hired whose families for generations had worked in Mexican silver mines. Laborers could work only short periods for fifteen to thirty minutes then were relieved by an alternate crew. A shaft reaching 3000' in depth had water registering 170°. By 1881 shafts were down to 4000' on the incline. There 180-190 miles of underground workings. Later, a large share of the men were foreign born. Could it have happened any other way, when two Irishmen were owners of the mine, that most of the miners were Irish.

SECRETS OF THE "TALKING WIRES"

Burro-prospectors were notorious for showing up within almost hours after a strike was made. Even when the discoverer had taken great pains to cover his tracks in his search and to get his ore assayed in the greatest secrecy. The word soon got out and a rush was on. At the Summit Diggings in the El Pasos, at Bullfrog with Shorty Harris, and at Gold Hill with O'Rielly—it was always the same. Just when a ray of sunshine shone glistening on yellow flakes in the pan the unfailing *sage-brush telegraph* spread the word and the gold-hungry boys came trooping in to locate claims all over the mountain.

When the cry of "*Gold* in the Washoe" spread through to the Mother Lode camps and in the stock market offices in San Francisco, any efforts to keep secrets were futile. As great sums of capital were raised by stock promotion schemes the need for secrecy was urgent. A chance rumor sent stocks sky-high or the bottom fell out, depending on the import of the message. A reliable telegraph line was needed as much as they needed water. Code words were agreed upon that would indicate conditions in the camps. Most famous of these systems was that used at the Comstock mines at Virginia City.

Code books were prepared using approximately 45,000 carefully selected code words. It enabled them to cover the whole range of language used in the conduct of mining activities, including those needed to participate on the floor of the Stock Exchanges of the cities. The "talking wires of Virginia City" never ceased day or night. Everything was boom or bust—"buy before the news gets out, they've struck a new lode on the 1200' level", or, "sell before they find out the shaft bottomed in worthless clay".

Each group had its own secret code books. They were given only to key personnel and kept in the safe. In some systems where economy of time or expense was needed number systems were developed representing key words or actions to be taken. It is reported that one code book had ten pages devoted to the subject of "ore" and more than two hundred code phrases under the heading of "mine". To further complicate a system, partners would by secret agreement, reverse the meaning of the words and phrases to confuse anyone in the company except the participants in the switch. It was reported that at one time, either in desperation or humer, there was a special code that read: "chuck steak" meant Ophir, "hash" meant Belcher, "mutton stew" referred to the Crown Point operation, etc. One code was developed that was described by the *Territorial Enterprise* as, "the most impenetrable contrivance hatched in the brain of mortal man."

SQUARE SET MINING

THE MINES

The development of the Comstock mine required new methods of extracting ores from great depths. Cave-ins, heat, and flooding were the principal hazards. Progress in this was made with the invention of new tools such as the compressed air drill, diamond-shaped rotary drill, and wire cables to replace the hemp rope lines.

The biggest problem in the Ophir Mine was the structure of the materials carrying the gold and silver ore and the adjacent walls. Problems developed that were completely new to miners' previous experiences. The Ophir ore body, which had been only ten to twelve feet wide on the fifty foot level, increased to forty to fifty feet in places on the 180 foot level. This was surrounded by materials so soft and unstable that no known method of timbering would permit its extraction without cave-ins. Ordinary cap and post were of no avail and pillars of ore left to act as supporting posts collapsed under the tremendous pressure.

The quartz ore was crushed and water-soaked. The surrounding walls were of clay and other decomposed materials. When an opening was made the whole country began to sag and swell as soon as it was exposed to air. In one area it kept filling in a large room as fast as men could wheel it out. This went on for several weeks before it was abandoned and the room was completely filled with the moving mass. A happy circumstance solved this problem when one of the mine owners discovered a young German engineer, Philipp Deidesheimer, who had worked in mines in California. He designed what became known as the "square-set method" of timbering that employed opposing wall forces to work against itself. Then framing and walls were added as the hole broadened.

As more and more ore was extracted conventional milling methods couldn't keep up. New mills with new ways of processing ore were built. In 1861 seventy-six mills were operating—some in Virginia City and Six-Mile Canyon below; many others in Gold Canyon from Gold Hill to the Carson River; a dozen along the Carson from Empire to Dayton; and seven more is Washoe Valley.

Better methods of transportation were needed between Virginia City and San Francisco. Freight and passengers had traveled by boat to Sacramento. From there it was a catch-as-catch-can affair. Thousands walked the makeshift road and trails. The more fortunate rode horses or in stage coaches. At the cost of half a million dollars a 101-mile toll road was built from Placerville to Virginia City. It was well graded and was macadamized. The daily traffic was unbelievable. It was an almost unbroken line of struggling, sweating mules hauling freight. Competing for road space was an endless number of stages and private wagons carrying passengers, mail, express and supplies.

Soon other roads crossed the Sierra to handle the traffic. By 1863-66 roads were built over Sonora Pass, Ebbett's Pass, Kit Carson Pass, and the Donner Pass. The most popular, the Placerville run of 101 miles was made in 12 hours! It was described as an exhilarating trip over the Sierras where six-horse stages trotted uphill and galloped madly downhill carrying passengers on their way to the Bay (San Francisco).

DIARY OF A BONANZA—THE COMSTOCK

1857: Discovery by two pick-and-shovel prospectors.

1864: The output of bullion doubled each year in the first three or four years.

1864-
1865: $16 million taken out.

1869: $7 million produced.

1879: Troubled times, stock was low. Smart investors began to sell—the unwary continued to buy. Hearst stock dropped from $1580 to $300 per "foot" in six months. Competing groups moved in to buy at a low figure. Such "bonanza kings" included Ralston (of the Bank of California) and James Flood. Business was maneuvered in Virginia City. People were bought out or squeezed out. Shares offered at $2.00 each went unsold.

1872: New interest took over. A determined search for new pockets were made during the next two years.

1873: Encouraging reports with new machinery which opened new areas. Shares selling for $1.00 in 1870 sold for $15.00 in 1872, and $700 in early 1875.

From 1874 to 1881 was the greatest production

1876 — $38 million	1879 — $7,500,000
1877 — $37 million	1880 — $4,300,000
1878 — $20 million	1881 — $1,400,000

1881: Costs were beginning to exceed returns.

1859-
1882: Total Production—$292,726,310.

*Surely there is a vein for the silver
and a place for gold where they fine it.*

— Job 28:1

GOLD FEVER—"An itch you can't scratch" was not limited to the "single-blanket-jackass" prospector. Today all through the Basin and Range country weekend prospectors are searching. Many find only cactus and rusty tin cans. Others hold communion with long gone dry-wash dreamers and envy their free-soul days when the search and its way of life was, in the end, to become its own reward.

The Gold Bonanza days are over but the search goes on. The largest producing gold mine in the United States is the mile deep Homesteak Mine at Lead, South Dakota. Hot mineral-bearing solutions formed its primary deposits that now produce over 575,000 ounces each year. In Nevada, at the Carlin Mine, the largest gold discovery of the past fifty years was opened in 1965. This was made following geologic investigations of the U.S. Geological Survey. An estimated $120 million in gold lies within the mountain.

In California's Mojave Desert, in December, 1977, a young man and his wife found a gold nugget with an exact weight of 156 ounces (about 13 pounds!)

SO, YOU WANT TO BE A PROSPECTOR?

Generally speaking vacant U.S. lands within the boundaries of national forests are open to "location" and entry for mining purposes under the general mining laws. subject to the jurisdiction of the U.S. Forest Service. Usually such operations are prohibited in National Parks or Monuments. Some exceptions are found where activity was allowed by precise exception in the original establishment of the national park or monument, such as at Death Valley.

1. To warrant filing any claim there must be strong evidence the area contains minerals in sufficient quantities and value to justify exploration. Neither *hope* nor expectation constitute a discovery.
2. All "grubstake" contracts are void unless written and properly recorded.
3. A "location" may be made without regard to the age, sex, or residence of the locator. Essential elements in locating either lode or placer claims are:
   a. discovery of mineral,
   b. marking the location boundaries,
   c. posting the Notice of Location,
   d. recording an exact copy at the County Recorder's office,
   e. posting the claim.

For a lode claim, mark at each corner of the claim and at the center of each end-line with a post not less than 4″ in diameter or a stone monument at least 18″ high. Early prospectors would often put their notice in a tin can and make it secure within a rock pile.

Placer claims should be marked so they can be legally traced. Early prospectors relied upon unwritten as well as written miner's law to make their claims secure in unsurveyed lands.

A good source for further information: any U.S. Forest Service office or the Division of Mines and Geology, Ferry Bldg., San Francisco for the latest in mining laws.

187

INDEX

In Appreciation ...

The writers would like to extend their thanks to the following people who have given their time and assistance in checking data, maps, and providing special photographs and other interpretative materials making this book as accurate, up-to-date and useful as possible.

Rocky Rockwell, Inyo National Forest, Bishop
Virgil Olsen, Naturalist, Death Valley National Monument
Matt & Rosemary Ryan, Former D.V. Ranger, Boulder City, Nevada
Ermine Stewart, Researcher, White Mountains National Forest, Bishop
Eleanor Leonard, California Division of Mines & Geology, San Francisco
Francilu Hansen, Desert Artist, Ridgecrest, California
Orion Marketing, Limited, Pismo Beach, California
The USGS Staff at Menlo Park and Reston, Virginia

LEW AND GINNY CLARK

Lew, a native son of a native daughter of California, grew up in Johannesburg when the Yellow Aster was stamping out gold ore daily. His father, Billy Clark was a teamster and operated the freight and stage route between Johannesburg and Skidoo. After acquiring his degree at Stanford, he taught history at all levels, from fourth grade to college. As a school administrator he worked in California, Idaho and Canada. His greatest joy was working as a backcountry Ranger in Yosemite and Grand Teton National Parks and as a Ranger Naturalist at Sequoia National Park and at Death Valley National Monument.

Ginny originally lived in New York State but immigrated to the golden west some thirty years ago. She was associated with such publishing firms as Harper & Row, Thomas Y. Crowell, Stanford University Press, and the San Francisco Chronicle. Being a mother of three kept her active before Western Trails Publications was established.

Together the Clarks have explored most of the fifty states, including Alaska, Canada, and Mexico. The guides they have written reflect a knowledge of the land and a concern about the care and conservation of our natural resources.

GUIDES by

LEW & GINNY CLARK ...

YOSEMITE TRAILS
JOHN MUIR TRAIL COUNTRY
MT. WHITNEY TRAILS
KINGS RIVER COUNTRY
HIGH MOUNTAINS & DEEP VALLEYS

All color photography and title page: Gold Point by Rocky Rockwell

BRISTLECONES ON WHITE MOUNTAIN (Front Cover)

THE ENVIRONMENTS (Inside Front Cover)

Shooting Stars up Pine Creek
Mojave Mound Cactus and Old Man
    Cactus in the Panamints
Joshua Tree on Inyo Mountains

Cresote in central Death Valley
Bristlecone of Schulman Grove
    in White Mountains
Eureka Dune Grass, Eureka Valley

THE LAND (Outside Back Cover)

Tinemaha Reservoir and Sierra Crest
Cerro Gordo Mountain and Mine
Death Valley, Panamints from
    Dantes View

Inyo Mountains
Southern Death Valley from Panamint
    Range (Striped Butte, center)
Sierra Crest from White Mountains

THE FLOWERS (Inside Back Cover)

Apricot Mallow
Old Man Cactus
Scarlet Locoweed

Panamint Daisy
Ranuncula
Mariposa Tulip